SPARROW ON THE PROPHET'S TOMB

SPARROW
ON THE
PROPHET'S
TOMB

THE CHRONICLES OF AKHIRA
MAULOOD
MECCA/MEDINA TIMEWARP

Daniel Abdal-Hayy Moore

The Ecstatic Exchange
2009
Philadelphia

For quotes any longer than those for critical articles and reviews,
contact:
The Ecstatic Exchange,
6470 Morris Park Road, Philadelphia, PA 19151-2403
email: abdalhayy@danielmoorepoetry.com

First Edition
ISBN: 978-0-578-02765-4 (paper)
Published by *The Ecstatic Exchange,*
6470 Morris Park Road, Philadelphia, PA 19151-2403

Also available from The Ecstatic Exchange:
Knocking from Inside, poems by Tiel Aisha Ansari

The hilye calligraphy on page 83, by Mohamed Zakariya, is used with his
permission.

Many of the poems in this book were published previously in the *Voices of
Islam* Series, Vincent J. Cornell, editor, Praeger, 2007.

Cover collage by the author (with thanks to photographer
Peter Sanders for use of palmtree background and Prophet's mosque)
Back cover photograph by Aburrahman Fitzgerald

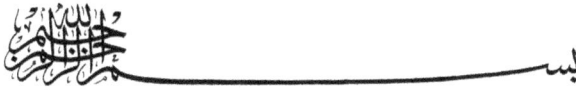

بسـ_____ ﷽

DEDICATION

To
Shaykh ibn al-Habib
(and the continuation of the Habibiyya)
Shaykh Bawa Muhaiyuddeen,
all shuyukh of instruction and ma'arifa
and
Baji Tayyaba Khanum
of the unsounded depths

and my companion journeyers...

_____

The earth is not bereft
of Light

CONTENTS

MECCA/MEDINA TIMEWARP

AUTHOR'S PREFACE

Of the three books collected here, the first is celebratory of Islam's eschatology (next-world doctrine), the second an homage to the Prophet Muhammad, peace and blessings of Allah be upon him, and the third written on an 'Umra in 1995/96 to Mecca and Medina.

The first one, *The Chronicles of Akhira*, was the first book of poetry I wrote after dissolving a nearly ten-year writing moratorium imposed by my then Sufi teacher, that happily opened floodgates which have been pouring fairly unabated since 1981 to today, in 2009. The poems imagine the Gathering on the Day of Rising, or Resurrection, and rather presumptuously continues to what it will be like in the Next World, written within its perspective, though based on God's word in the Qur'an and statements and descriptions by the Prophet, as well as lore and tidbits picked up along the way by variously inspired teachers, including, most importantly, the great shaykh's collection of songs, the Diwan, of Muhammad ibn al-Habib of Fez.

The poems that make up *The Chronicles of Akhira* and *Maulood*, come from a time when I had lived in intensified isolation from the rest of the world in various Muslim/Sufi communities in Britain and America, and it may be somewhat instructive to know that when one is isolated to establish "religious" and spiritual tenets among equally intense co-religionists, one tends to see things in strong contrasts, the spiritual goal versus the rest of the world, and perhaps be sterner rather than sweeter, generally, basing one's views on definitively and strongly held positions.

The book, *Maulood*, written in 1984, is an honoring of the Prophet Muhammad, while cognizant of the West's difficulty in assessing him from our cultural context, and so is an attempt to get at both his glory and spirituality from what I found in the years of visiting saints and adepts around the world, attempting to translate that to both an alien and alienated populace. Hence its seeming struggle to find the right images and words that would correspond to western associations, to delineate a man who is both familiar to us in his human aspect but unfamiliar in his being the Prophet and God's Messenger, since for us prophets are either Old Testament desert ascetics, or modern religious innovators of often dubious lineage. And Jesus (or Sayyedina 'Isa for Muslims, peace be upon him), has been theologically elevated beyond "mere" prophethood throughout Church history, thus making it more difficult to limn the (in fact) vast, exalted and coterminously sanctified stature of prophethood by Muslim standards.

The third book, *Mecca/Medina Timewarp,* was written more recently, poems from an 'Umra, or Lesser Visit, to Mecca and Medina, at the turn of the year, 1995/96, and contains the title poem of this volume, which has become somewhat familiar to Muslim audiences in both England and America (the Yemeni shaykh, Habib Ali Jaffri, incorporated it into his talk at a Mawlid in England when he rose to speak). Regarding the series of poems, I intended to write poems *in situ* at the Ka'ba and at the Prophet's mosque, in the time-honored tradition of various literary and scholarly visitors to these sacred sites.

These are all poems of my root work, going down into the loam of study, practice and fidelity to the ideas and often the terminology of Islamic and Sufic thought, while my poetic development since these books incorporates more imaginally leaping imagery and unhesitantly associational language, to more openly circumscribe both the tone and experience of a modern American but cosmopolitan Muslim/ Sufi in our very promising but rambunctiously tumultuous times.

SONG WRITTEN BEFORE THE PROPHET
by Shaykh ibn al-Habib al-Amghari al-Idrisi al-Hasani

Here we sit in the *rawdah* bathed in the Prophet's presence
Seeking divine satisfaction and a beautiful welcome

We have come to you needy, O safest of refuges,
Broken, brought low, and bewildered to the core

Ask God to grant us every goodly care
To reward our hopes at the moment of Resurrection

The clarity of your power and incomparable message
Surpasses those of every sent Messenger

You are God's gateway to every good
And whoever reaches you finds satisfaction and reunion

Every secret from the prophets has proceeded
From your sublime station, affirmed by transmission

I plead my case through Your Prophet, O God,
From Your promise to accept his intercession

All who encamp at the abode of a generous host
Attain their most fervent wish and everything they seek

So here we thank God for every blesséd time
He grants us a visit to our beloved Messenger

And every time we visit the graveyard at Baqi

And all the Companions and Fatima's children

And each time we visit the wives and daughters
And son of humanity's rescuer at that fateful Day

And every time we visit those who fell at Uhud,
The noble martyrs and the Prophet's uncle

By virtue of their rank, we ask for supreme safety
On our journey home and when we enter into it

And for safe deliverance on the Day of Gathering
And to guard us from every crassly ignorant fool

O my Lord, bless the Prophet and his entire Family
And Companions and Followers who emulate his qualities

(This song was recited by the shaykh in the "rawdah" in front of the Prophet's tomb in Medina, and copied by a companion. "Rawdah" from the hadith: "Between my minbar and my grave is a rawda from among the riyaad of Heaven," also meaning "garden" or "meadow." This version is based on translations made by Aisha Tarjumana, with help from Abdarrahman Fitzgerald and Shakir Masoud.)

THE CHRONICLES OF AKHIRA

1981

---

with typoglifs by Karl Kempton

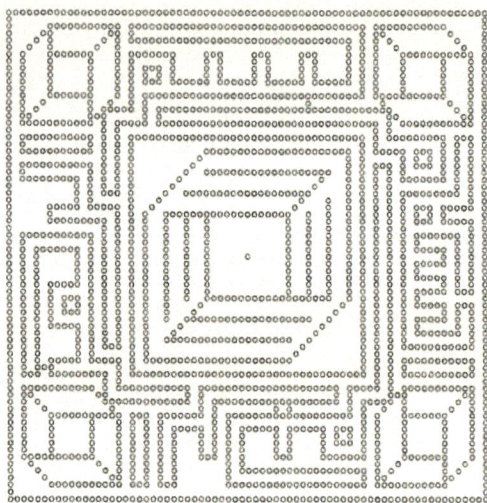

PREFATORY NOTE

The word *akhira* is Arabic, meaning, *"the last, the end,"* and so by extension, in Islamic cosmology, the Next World, the last world in the chain of creation that extends beyond death. For us, there is no reincarnation in this world. This world is only a phase, and not even the first phase of our passage as human individuals.

The picture is five-fold. First, pre-eternity, before our particular creation, a time when everyone in subtle form recognized and acknowledged the One True Invigorator of everything: *Allah*, since in that state we as well were unified, and so had little difficulty perceiving Him, may He be exalted. The second phase is the nine months, more or less, in the wombs of our mothers. After that period comes everyone's decreed lifespan on earth, each one unique. After death, there is an undetermined time in the grave, enjoyable or terrible according to our behavior in the previous world that constitutes the field of actions. Then comes the fifth phase, the Day of Rising, when the graves open up, and, in our own bodies, but unlike their present material form, we are gathered on a vast plain. This experience is prepared for in this world by the Muslims on the Hajj to Mecca when they gather two-million (plus) fold and dressed identically in two lengths of white cloth, on the plain of 'Arafat, which in Arabic means: *Recognition*. On this endless, featureless plain in the Next World, we are judged, again according to our actions, and conducted either to the Fire or to the Garden, to remain in them forever. According to some scholars, however, even eternity, as part of Allah's creation, is finite, and so it too is annihilated at last, until the only remaining existence is the Face of Allah.

Now, it is an astonishing thing to think that after so many millenniums of human life, in which people had knowledge of the dimension of the Afterworld, we have "evolved" a highly sophisticated society that both knows virtually nothing about it, often by a kind of wayward intellectual choice (having decided beforehand that it does not exist), and actually living in terror of even the notion of a world after death. And the so-called "culture" of the West only supports this blank both in regards to the after-death state and death itself. What is most moving and tragic about the people in the movie "Terms of Endearment" is not the inevitable event of death itself, but rather the total lack of anyone's knowing what to think or say about it, or what to expect, and the terrible, cold uneasiness in the face of it on the part of everyone. The family surrounds the victim dying of cancer with nervous small-talk, and at the end, the victim goes to death with no response to her last words from anyone present, all asleep or inattentive in the chairs of her hospital room. A lonely and ignorant experience, in this Age of Technological Wonders.

This is the situation we find ourselves in today vis-a-vis the Unseen, or the Next World, almost completely. It is an identical situation to the one the Prophet Muhammad, peace be upon him, encountered in Mecca, when he faced the idol-worshippers of his day. They said, "What, when we die are we not just bones and dust? How can we be brought back to life again?" meaning, after the grave. But sophistication will not save us. No amount of totally efficient plastic kitchens will keep the Next World from opening up to us at last, but the worst thing will be the ignorance and surprise felt by the citizens going into it. It would be better to be at least a little prepared, or at least disposed to admit its existence, when it is then too late to deny it. This is the dimension in which we are identical to the Communist, atheistic world, which insists that such a reality simply does not exist (too dangerous for the Industrial State). But all man has to do is regard his dream world to realize there is something more to existence than steamrollers and supermarkets. The turning to alcoholism, as in Russia today, is always a sign of a thwarted inner life, just as it is for the Native American Indian, deprived of his or her contact with the Unseen by an obfuscating socio-spiritual doctrine that replaces their natural, subtle and majestic truth by a boorish, ignoble lie both in vision and practice.

This poem is based on a living, existentially accessible doctrine which in its prime sources is vivid and detailed, and *complete*. The description of the Next World, neither vague clouds and harps, nor the monstrous, many-armed djinn of the awe-inspriring Tibetan cosmology, is simple and breathtaking, and has close affinities with the visions people revived from a coma state often have, when they are able to describe them. These are not, by the way, people who are dead then alive, for their decree of death was obviously not for that time, but in the depth of their coma state they may have had a taste of that Other World, and in coming back fully into this one they were able to describe, or hint at, certain specific phenomena.

On the Day of Gathering we are all brought together, each one of us. There are no nationalities then, no races, but only the states of the hearts of those gathered. Everyone is there, from the time of Adam to the last person on earth. We re-inhabit our bodies, but now of subtler stuff, and the blind, deaf, and dumb, as well as those without limbs, have all their missing senses and parts restored, although the Qur'an says that the spiritually blind in this world will be struck "physically" blind in the Next World as well.

After the Day of Gathering there is the separating out of those for the Fire and those for the Garden, just as in alchemical smelting; that which is pure is separated from that which needs to pass through a further process of purification. Then there is a bridge, described in this poem, over which we all must pass, easily and swiftly for some, slowly and laboriously for others, some not even managing to cross, the flaming Fire licking beneath it. Some fall in. The fortunate cross over. On the opposite side lies the Garden of bliss, trees of shade, feasting and reclining, and ease and sweetness, while in the hells are those whose states were hellish or whose actions were irredeemably awful and solid. Dante's descriptions of Hell and his system of Heaven were at least inspired by Latin versions of either the hadith literature of the Prophet of Islam, peace be upon him, or the works of the great Spanish Muslim Shaykh of the 12th century (Christian Era), Muhyiuddin Ibn al-'Arabi, translations of which were circulating in Europe at the time Dante wrote his *Commedia*.

There is one episode early in the poem that recalls the meeting of world powers, almost all related to Queen Victoria, to map out the territories belonging to their respective nations, across Europe and Africa. This refers to the present world, hemmed in by passport borders and police-state rigidity, fostering a narrow nationalism, when the fact is that all people are from the Tribe of Adam, can communicate the most refined notions to one another, and will all be brought together at last on the Day when the ultimate Balance is set up.

The important thing to know is that this is a living tradition, the news is fresh and detailed, and was brought to us by a trustworthy Messenger, Muhammad, peace and blessings of Allah be upon him, whose name means "the praised one," who praised Allah in every state, and was in turn praised by Him, the figure of relief who appears at the end of this chronicle, without whose existence the means to this knowledge would have eluded us completely. One fourth of the earth's population knows this as true, and it is the balm to soothe our sophisticated fright into peaceful awareness beyond the confines of what is, in fact, really just a short passage in time: *our life*.

———————————————

(Note: Decipherment of the calligraphic typoglifs can be found on page 78)

THEY CAME DOWN FROM THE HIGH AND LOW PLACES,

they threaded themselves along
    through the intricate threadings,
the ancient ones and the new ones,
all the famous were among them,
    all the shining stars,
all the historical glory-grabbers, the great thieves,
all the inventors with their psychological quirks,
the nobodies came as well, the flowing multitudes of the anonymous,
the endless dissatisfied housewives, authoritative bureaucrats,
    gas-station attendants and couples with no children,
philanthropists and the workaholics,

they came through the sandy pass,
faces were indistinguishable, differences unnoticed,
naked they came and assembled,
fear for their own state kept their eyes on the ground,

they came and made ranks,
the noble and notable next to the hardened criminal,
    the saint in his glow next to the shrew in her darkness,
all the Chinese came, all the Australian Aborigines,
some who had never been clothed came,
and some who had never been out of them,

important socialites were bereft of their diamonds,
the scholar with references bereft of his briefcase,
the policeman with his beer-belly pitched on his heels,
the priest with his miter now gone, lost in a haze,

well-known faces recognized in the earthly crowd
were lost in the mass now, shaded by the one standing next to it,
no Rolls-Royce stood ready for the king,
    his feet made dust-prints with the rest,
no helicopter hovered to take the millionaire away,
    he felt the weight of his reconstituted body now with the rest,

as they awaited the setting-up of the scales,
as humanity assembled on the plain under a blinding sun
and awaited the judgment to fall

that would decide each one's place.

Even the sainted were afraid, the ones whose hearts
    glowed like a sunrise
through the transparency of their rib-cages,
even they were covered in sweat to their eyebrows,
the camel-drivers of the edge,
the caravan-leaders at the margins of the earth,
the destitute, delicate, daring hearts who
    stayed up nights calling out in hope
and spiritual derangement,

they took their places in this place of no-place
and awaited the click that would tell all,
    the sinking or rising of the pan
with the light or heavy scales registering
        the forever of their moments
            lengthened out now along a line

visible from the beginning to the end of each life

like a straight narrative, or a string with knots in it.
No flaws in the universe,
and the universal memory has no lapses.

Each dwarf or giant of sensibility and care
came to the jamboree

at the beginning of Eternity
and wondered in its echoes

what its final fate would be.

TIMETABLE 1

All the historical pantomimes
that spelled out subtitles in fractured rhymes
under the movie that unrolled forwards or backwards
were resolved in a blink by the spark of the falling swords
as they clanged into the tree-trunk at the end of time
to signal the cut-off point of the nonsensical pantomime.

A large round table in a large square hall
where men in uniforms stood before their fall
and unrolled a map of the world laid flat
and passed a pencil from one hand — fat
and pudgy with excess of pork in their diet —
to another to draw outlines in a universal riot
of borders and frontiers and nationalities crazed,
then shook hands and sniffed importantly,
    leaving the peasantry dazed
for decades in hemmed-in contraptions of death
that counted off heartbeats and charged rent for each breath.

Kaisers and kings and presidents and führers,
shoulder to shoulder under portraits of ancestors
in a chandeliered hall in Vienna, Austria,
an old world country with shelves full of china
and invisible cobwebs behind beer-mugs and plates,
and visible dust on the map of new states
as they left the table to the drawing-room cigar
as flames caught its edges and began the scar
that ran its wound through the human heart
separating mankind into one cubby-holed part

next to another, like several square pigeon-coops set on the globe
as it turns slowly eastward in its cloud-lined robe.

The life of this world
is just a series of skeletons dancing in the dark.

The life of this world
is a series of skeleton keys opening different doors.

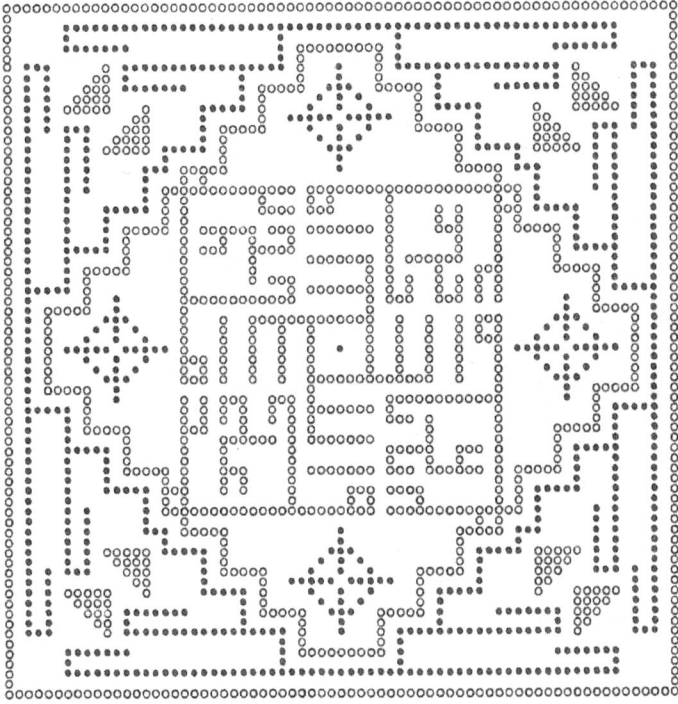

THE FEW WITH ELEGANT MANNERS

The few with elegant manners came as if alighting from horses,
they stepped down and gathered folds of radiance around them
as their feet hit the ground which showed no footprint below them
    for it was not solid ground beneath them
        — the footprints in dirt were for those
           who saw it as gross and solid beneath them —

they went on, straight-backed, to their places
and stood patiently waiting, but their waiting was bird-flight,
    wings in the wind, all the flurry of wing-tips that ever
        flew in the world down below
    fanned now in the air of their waiting.

Their faces were moons assembled on cloudless horizons,
their eyelids were shields drawn down over inward gazes,
their hands rested at their sides, relaxed and pulsing,

    no terror shook them, as promised,
    no last-minute griefs or regrets,
    no sudden anxieties to go back to do something differently.

They cast no shadows as the sun bore down upon them,
    shaded by the Throne that stood
        immaterially before them.

These were the Chosen Ones.

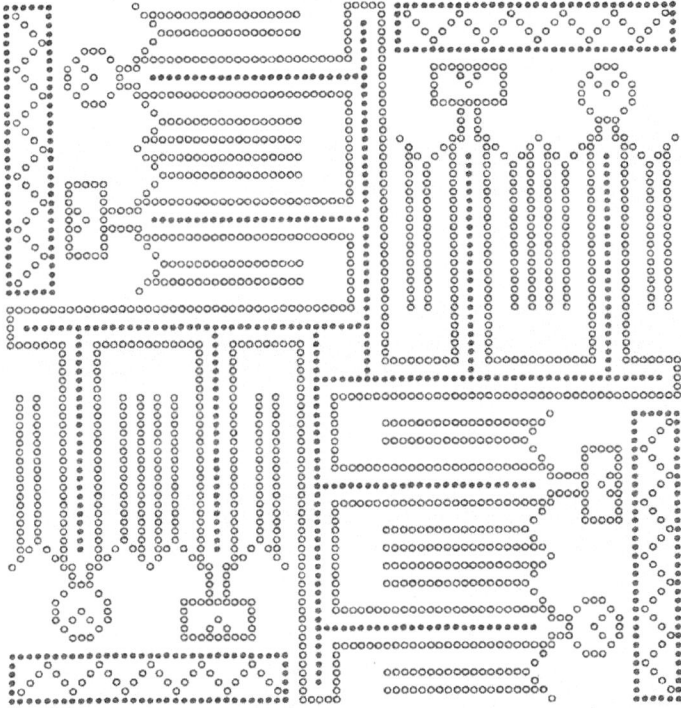

EVERYONE HAD SET OUT

Everyone had set out on the journey to Allah,
the historical records are complete
   down to the last detail.

Some of them died of thirst in a dry place,
some of them drowned in the abundance that splashed
  its fruity suds in excess
    in this unique universe full of stars.
Some reached the goal of their search in a shoot-out on a
     back street in Chicago.
Some in alchemical laboratories engulfed in the *blue flash!*
Some rode alongside railroads with sacks of money
  on perspiring horses.
Some in a quiet lounge in an overstuffed chair
   reading newspapers.

Some had their hearts cut out and offered to the sun,
and so found their destiny and its knowledge
sticking them between the ribs with its obsidian edge.
Some lost their head as they reached the peak
  but froze their feet.

All sought the God Who created them,
Who is not in hiding behind some far-away cloud,
but is nearer than our jugular vein
and the Answerer to our call.

Everyone took the torturous journey
and here they stand.

To look at them you wouldn't know
who or what they lavished such affection on,
what they adored and how,
     except that the shifting, anxious eyes tell all,
the nervous looking for escape routes
now that the impending finale of all the spontaneous charades
     is closing upon them,
and the photo-albums fall open around their feet
displaying all the gods and bit-players
     they gave honor to, and dressed in halos and crowns
and presented with emotional ticker-tape parades
and agonized over in the dark of night,

the family portraits with the grim benefactor stiff-necked behind
but the awaiting recipients of his benefactions pretending
     innocence in the front row,
not relying on the Original Source for all
          beneficence.

To judge only outwardly,
the few skulls and thigh-bones left in the earth,
the broken teeth and occasional evidence of a
     sharp blow with a dull weapon,
or footprints which might tell a tale of erect posture
     or a hunting or homesteading instinct,
all these outward tokens do not attest to the

twists and turns of the journey each of them took

to get here
to this place

at last.

The volumes of utterance attest —
some like cries heard from the mouth of a well,
some like contented singing on a slow river-bank,
some like the true weeping of solitude's friend
who sees the shore from which his root was wrenched loose
    and longs for a return —

these voices attest in their burble to the true gamble
each one took to find the God of them all.

Each heart is burning
and each tongue makes sparks
    in the dark night.

These fragments fluttering through the library corridor
and down the evacuated stairwell
like whispers and moans of these voices now
    silent in the boneless, non-historical bodies
reconstituted on this endless plain
under a blistering sun, a murderous sun —
    in this fully attended gathering
        down to the dead-at-infancy,
these fragments like tape-recordings of the whole forest jabber
    of humankind's mad desire

to be reunited to the One —

it stands out now, unrolls,
thunder cracks all across it,

the vocal orchestra up-heaves
like a tidal flood of heart's desire,
the speech of heartbeats made verbal
against the silent, silent sand.

Mouths of Napoleons are gaping,
    no words come out.

Eyes of Caesars are round,
    they see nothing.

The crowd is immense,
and like fleas on an elephant,
the individual characteristics of each
are lost against the gray bulk.

But each hour-glass filled with actions like sand
is tipped to fall through each individual's hand.

Each hand-print will be different on the sand-pattern sealed
by the actions they made in the terrestrial field.

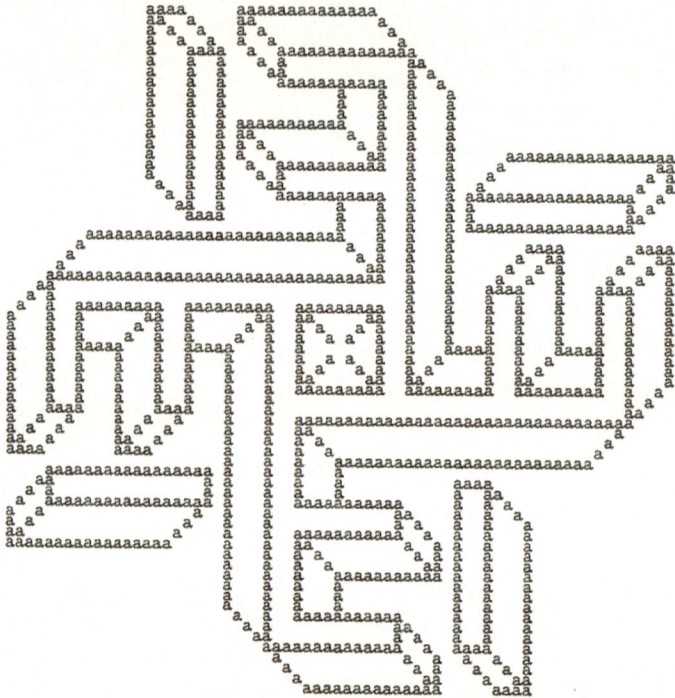

HOW DID THEY KNOW

How did they know Who they were looking for
and why did He come in such different disguises?
First, because they all saw Him before,
before they assumed their physical sizes.

Arrayed in ranks before worlds were born,
they saw with their eyes and testified.
Then they fell into swoons of birth
and in life some laughed while others cried.

But then, at that moment, He appeared, full Light,
and no one missed His Face or Voice.
But trails and roads and thorny ways
then faced each one with multiple choice.

Some chose darkness, it was in their genes,
some chose fog or the gray, wet mist.
Some went to light like iron to magnets,
and some regretted the life they had missed.

Some forgot for a second or two,
others for years until the last breath took,
then on their pillows they suddenly saw
and the final spasm their whole being shook.

But that moment was enough for the mirror to fill
with vast light without form or intensity,
for them to swim like a mote in air
into the immensity of immensity.

Then ones who never forgot for a second
put shoes on with wings on and flew across earth.
They sang the different hues of the rainbow
and saw in their death a secret rebirth.

The pendulum swung between dark and light,
terror and bliss, disaster and good,
but they only saw Him, that Original Face,
in whatever smile or executioner's hood.

They never left that original spot
in ranks in rows for miles before Him.
Their beings always reverberated
and never stopped learning how to swim.

Like a lighthouse beam, their boats zeroed in
on the ray that falls on waves and rocks,
but the waves and rocks are illusory forms
just as time is not measured by mechanical clocks

but by breaths blown across space by the Spirit of Light
in cyclic rhythms that rise and fall,
and we float like molecules turning in air
through the entirely empty emptiness of it all.

For inside our forms the molecules packed
right next to each other are cosmic spheres
we could travel inside of and not touch matter
for absolutely millions of years.

That first space floats like bell-sound inside us

struck at the start by the Creator's touch,
and the echo of our recognition of Him,
face to face, is what inspires us such

to set out on the journey, the return-trip home —
we all have return-trip tickets to Him.
Each breath is pre-paid, and our heartbeat passports
are a sure way to the purest Presence of Him.

But He's given us each a different airline,
different psychological stewardesses too.
Some serve alcohol, some vegetarian,
some like the "good time" while others are "blue."

So He has to appear in a way we will see
or we'll miss Him entirely in the kaleidoscope crowd,
but we never miss Him, He is always there
in the first white diaper or the last white shroud.

An edge, a bit of the picture, for some,
a name scrawled on notepaper scrunched in the pocket,
a telephone number, but forget who it's for,
a light bulb that won't fit into any light-socket.

Some go along shoeless, bereft of the feast
they heard about years ago but can't find the door.
Others have never left the table,
for them the sky is the same as the floor.

They see the clouds go by in the steps they take
in any direction they happen to choose.

Then when He appears to them, Light upon Light,
this molecular map they are ready to lose.

The best go to Him in original form,
just affirmation with no tongue to speak,
pure *yes's* pounding like pulses upon them,
echoed and multiplied, peak upon peak.

They sit like mirrors on icy mountains,
empty, frameless, motionless space,
and suspend all thought and breath and desire
just to reflect His Eternal Face.

No climb got them there, no fall made them fall,
they never left their original spot
on subways or diners, street corners, cabs,
in whatever shape of the Potter's pot

they happened to be formed in, handle and spout.
And then at the last, they went singing — *out!*

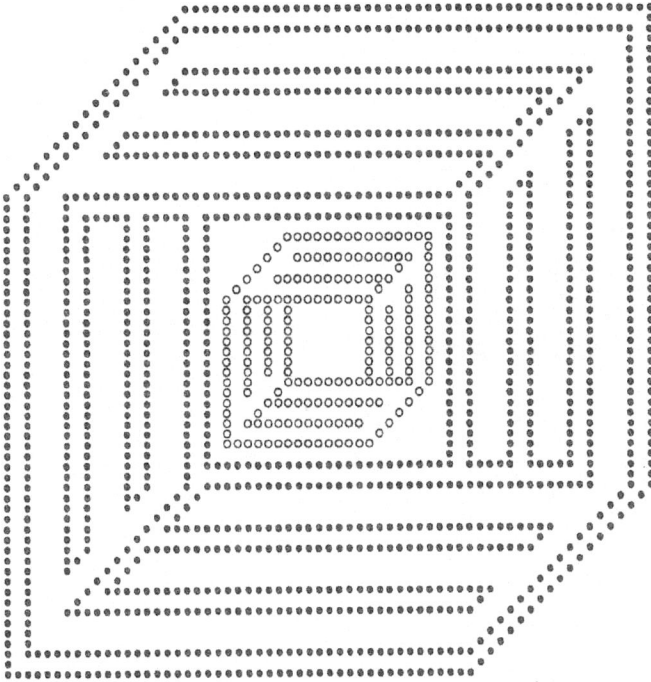

TIMETABLE 2: The Biographical Farewell

The bathtub water grew cold around him
as he lay soaking, stunned, at the prospect of The End.
He wanted to be clean, he wanted to relax, he
    didn't know what to want or stop wanting,
or what he would do in the next
       forty-eight hours,

the yellow smoke rushing in from all corners of the sky now
like blasts from a steam-whistle,
and the lightning playing across the night
    like pick-up sticks
       in a losing game.

Forty-eight hours, and all the bridges down.

He contemplated his naked body stretched out before him,
the one he always had and always ended up with
  at last, how it had changed, stomach
flattening and bulging, leg-muscles slackening,
red knees like lily-pads, water in little eddies around them

and nowhere to run to.

All the old securities, the office-building with its aura
    of permanence,
  granite blocks piled up on quicksand,
the family gathering probably gaping into mirrors just like
      he was now
hardly able to swallow

because of the numb shock of it,
the gut-feeling of actual disintegration
        taking place on a mass scale
with no thunder-rolls to orchestrate its demise.

The sky out the window looks like fire on the wing of a
        World War II biplane
spinning into the sea.

What's above is turning down below, what's below is
        Ferris-wheeling around, and the
ground is rocking.

He's flowing backwards.
Bedrooms and wallpaper flash through his mind
        a frame at a time,
smiles, waves, figures by rosebushes,
        goldfish on bookcases,
embarrassments and apologies, caught red-handed
        in the dark,
the private hells replayed on a fast machine,

flying backwards with stellar debris
pouring into his openings,
mouth filling with dust,
eyes filling with cloud-trails,
ears hearing the high-pitched shriek,

in a bathtub at the age of two,
a basinet at the age of one,

in the womb at the age of none

back to the One.

Laid out in his naked body stretched before him,
the one he always had and always ended up with,

wrapped in white cloth like a banana skin,
skeleton sealed in a white cloud

laid under the sun.

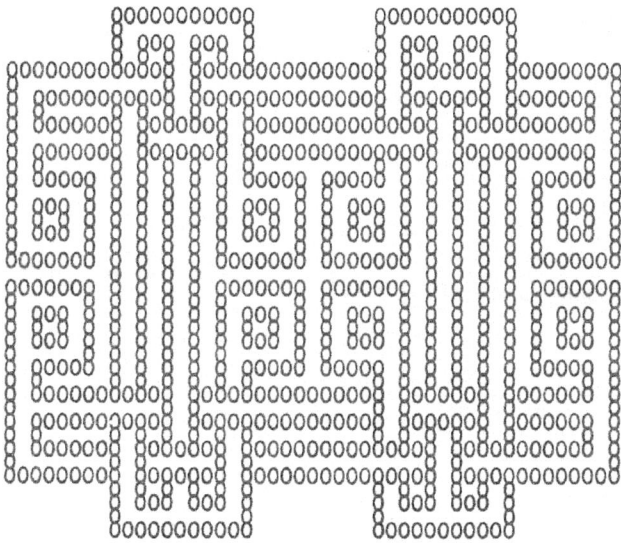

TIMETABLE 3

Man is a little cosmos.
The cosmos is a big man.
— Sufi saying

A great milk beard has spread over the earth,
    scorpions hiding in its hairs —
a great milk beard extends down the naked body of the earth
    stretched out in its bathtub of stars.

Nostradamus stands with one squinting eye
    making peculiar proclamations —
some could be the corner of a cube
    visible from the fourth dimension,

some just Technicolor voodoo.

Chinese acrobats spell out Taoist phrases
    on a field of blue poppies
and all the audience applauds.

A Hindu swami up to his waist in mud
    for a hundred years of silence
opens cadaverous jaws
    and yawns.

Jehovah's Witnesses burn calendar pages
    with the red-letter day of
doom for the hundredth time
    making it a part of their ceremony in their

collapsing tabernacle in black snow.

Scandinavians fill socks with painted eggs
    and fall out of windows
in suicide due to over-liberation.

Balinese click their eyes from side to side
    in subtle deep-forest trance-dances
balancing trays full of magnolia petals
    to the funeral of their paper idol.

Spaniards sit out in the blazing sun
    playing dominos in a dirt parking lot
with a scratchy radio blaring.

Catholics wait in audience
    while the Pope sits heavily guarded
on a gold toilet seat
    while the Amazon Indian parish

perishes of tuberculosis due to
    vitamin deficiency in a
heavy rain.

Communists file by their leader
    held in suspended animation
in a glass box between two
    total disintegrations but

unable to go to either
    in his waxen mask, neither

to this world nor the next.

Bahai's hold hands in universal brotherhood
    while Israel pays for a mausoleum
to house their leader in Tel Aviv
    by a mountainside of forgotten Torahs,

burnt Bibles and acid-eaten Qur'ans.

Zen Buddhists incline toward a wall,
    incline toward a wall, incline toward a wall
while the traffic snarls outside
    on their lonely mountaintop in samadhi.

Jews ask servants to switch on electric lights on Saturday
    and drive their cars and open their doors
on the Sabbath free from all kinds of manual labor.

Official Muslims in little silver slippers
    step down from black mafia limousines
onto rainbow-colored roulette-wheels
    where they are slowly turned,

dripping in their own fat,
    on the rotisserie of the Eternal Barbecue.

Americans wash the holy automobile
    with suds whose giant bubbles contain pictures
of refrigerators and knife-sharpeners and religiously haloed
    electric toothbrushes that blow away in the late

morning breeze under the squeegee's
    monotonous squeak.

Great processions circle the United Nations
    with plastic umbrellas embossed with gold leaf
designations of each major religion as they assemble
    for the Freemason's jamboree in a hall packed with

black balloons and indecipherable insignias.

The rain of atomic weaponry falls in a slant
    down the distant backdrop but barking dogs
herald the arrival of the blimp
    carrying the Head of State,

a disembodied monologue of moving lips
    no one heeds.

The projector runs the historical movies
    from international archives at double speed —
throws in a mercury flash,
    gold dust and a smell of burning flesh —

backwards to the great dusty crowds jeering
    at the newly-arrived Prophet as he speaks,
making eyes at each other and clucking noises
    with their tongues waiting to rush him

with fistfuls of rocks,
    as the white-cloaked followers close in
around him to rush him off

to some quiet place

at the end of time
    at last.

A great white beard has sprouted
    from head to toe along the earth's
naked body
    as it lies in a tub

turning colder by the second
    swerving mightily through the ocean of stars.

The mouth under the moustache is still.

The night is a slow line.

WHEN THE CURTAIN CLOSES

When the curtain closes on this world
it opens on the other side.
All the pictures and innermost fantasies
slip down the final landslide

and the voyage begins for the lover
as he sees the crystal lakes
spread out before him in tranquility
in an air that no shout breaks.

The bridge like a rainbow arches
flinging its arc across fire
and sets one down on a musk cloudbank,
epitome of all desire.

Each glimpse of love or roses
in this world was Polaroid,
instant snapshot that yellows,
a shadow on celluloid,

a profile passing a window,
then gone in a purplish smoke.
Ecstasy soon turns sour
and sublimity into a joke.

But there, past the portals of Light,
nothing transient is allowed to remain.
Eternity grows there, it flowers,
it floods in a constant rain

and love-flights and ecstasies vanquish
each vanishing tremble or quake,
and you sit in pure contemplation
of the Face of Allah, for *His* sake.

On balconies ranged in pure space now
the slave like a light flash beams
and watches the works of creation
like the floating machinery of dreams.

The dynasties pass like a thought
with the boisterous, tumultuous crowds,
their moments of epic history
like dark spots on fast-moving clouds.

Wisps of worlds unweave their threads
of smoke on a vacant screen
and drift in different directions
like something only half-seen

the rest imagined, badly reported,
cataloged in cabinets of snow
that melt with their data inside them
back to the Knower of all there is to know,

all the moments ticked like a time clock,
trooped back to Original Source,
full four-dimensional arenas of action
now the size of the twitch on a horse

which gallops for five hundred years

under a tree slowly spreading its shade,
but never reaches the end of it
in this immaterial glade

that opens out on a river
of whispers whooshing to sea
where worlds are suspended in a tear-drop
that slides down the cheek of "To Be,"

and disappears! All this theater
from balconies ranged in the air
is seen from the vantage of emptiness
where there's no room for even one hair.

As everything sinks, light rises
in this going-on place past the veil,
a place where nothing at all happens
that doesn't happen like wind in a sail

blowing nowhere. But no boredom,
no tedium strikes one there,
the energies fall in full flight forward
through an air that is nothing like air

nor even like nothing.
It's the opposite to everything here.
We walk through the grave like a doorway
into time without minute or year.

We wait in the ground for the angels
to come in their monstrous fanged masks,

and answer without hesitation
what each of them urgently asks.

Then a door at grave's end flashes open
that shows us our place in the shade
on the green, green hills of the Garden
under trees of the pure light we made

by our trust and belief each second,
when seconds were counted like grains
that sifted so quickly through fingers
busy measuring losses and gains.

Then one day, or century, trumpets
are blasted like one violent quake
and split open graves by their noise
and up we spring like a snowflake

drifting so weightlessly earthward —
in the same way we float to our feet.
New bodies of subtle light clothe us,
our mouths are all bitter, or sweet.

We assemble on deserts of space
as naked as we were born
and wait in the heat for the judgment
to pass like a firing-squad's morn.

One shot and it's over — *the moment.*
To Fire or Garden we go.
Faces in gloom burst and blacken

while others are shining like snow.

A river of light bathes our quirks off,
the last bits we brought from this life,
and on opposite banks of velvety ferns
we are reunited with wife

or husband, and children, beauty and stars,
the orbiting planet around us.
We cross the bridge to the Garden like bursts
of the lightning-bolt that found us

in the womb on earth, that split-second meeting
of sperm and egg in the dark.
Now we meet the spiritual circle
in which we are just one more spark

flying high in the beaks of green birds,
mountain-peaks passing slowly below,
rivers of honey and milk and music
lengthening out in a slow

majestic single note held long,
just one note sounded alone.
The one flute by the One flute-player
Who has reconstructed, bone by bone

and connection by connection
a body of bliss buoyed by air
that has no place to be in,
no "*nowhere*" nor no "*where*."

The cycle arches to endlessness,
circular loops in His space,
and in each turn or twist of the fabric,
the perfect Light of His Face.

His Face! His One Face without features,
lovers lose life in its search!
But now all hearts are embraced by it,
and no one is left in the lurch.

The cursed are tasting the bitterness,
the blessed are drinking the sweet.
The Light of His Face is bathing
each body from our heads to our feet.

No attributes of humanity
remain with these beings of Light
on the other side where we end up
which in this world is just out of sight.

Nothing that can be spoken of,
no song can reach that state.
No silence can even suggest it,
nor anything snarled in fate.

Endlessness, pure, without limits!
Moments that have no sphere!
Light that has no incandescence!
A *"there"* that has nothing of *"here!"*

DIARY OF ONE OF THE RESIDENTS OF AKHIRA

1st Day

I am not really writing this, but if I were it would go something like this. There is no need to record what happens here. For whom? It is all undifferentiated radiance of varying shades like an aurora borealis shuddering ceaselessly over a flat white plain. And it is not at all like this.

One cannot see a horizon. There is no stopping-point for one edge and starting-point for another. Earth does not touch sky here, sky does not sit on earth. This was the first thing I noticed.

We were given our accommodations. Great glass-like globes nested in hillsides of musk, with rooms of circular chambers, the insides visible at times from the outside, although, like a kind of opaque film or slight storm passing through their surfaces, they cloud over from time to time and become solid spherical walls.

I am used to my new body in an amazing way. Things pass through it quite easily, and it passes through things. It has a greenish tint. The bones are like glass tubing one can see through. The blood, if it *is* blood, circulates in a kind of visible flutter through the webbing of capillaries, but this may all be just a memory of my previous body, and has nothing at all to do with my present one. There is no way of telling.

We watched great turquoise and silver orbs rise past the farthest distance (it was the first time I could perceive a kind of edge to the space here), and cross over above us, then go down at an opposite point. Someone said they were the desires of ages long past which had solidified as planetary masses and appeared from time to time here for the enjoyment of the residents. Their colors shone on everything, beams shooting through the transparency like light down a glass rod.

There is no bumping into things. No weight. No awkwardness.

Everything is a meaning, a sudden, comprehensible picture that shines its significance into the heart. Nothing goes by that is not part of the whole.

There is no fatigue.

2nd Day

Coming down a stairway of cloud onto a bank the consistency of white bread, stepping onto a floor of light as if from a horse or pack-animal, standing squarely in space with arms spread and legs firmly planted, head like a wind-tunnel or library of voices echoing out of distant caves, the soft moan and cry of everyone sang through my tongue!

There is no praise or prayer, there is no forgetfulness or separation. It is Himself praising Himself, and Himself viewing Himself, and no one else is here, can be said to be here, or hiding, but the One Presence. Prayer would be forgetfulness. Here it is the opposite to the first world — forgetfulness there might have led you to the Fire.

There is a place nearby that is open, and you can hear the cries of the people in the Fire yelling for water, for just one drop of water to refresh them from the steam and boiling cauldrons of their heads. But we are powerless to pour any down, and it would do no good to them anyway. It would only make things worse. But they can see us, and we can see them. It must be awful to be able to see us, but not come to where we are.

What kept me from that place when I acted in the world was such a slight thing! But here I can see how great a gulf separates us, as it always did, and how what I did there seemed small, but was the difference between acting for the Garden and acting for the Fire. There is no comparison.

3rd Day

Pure contemplation. We went to a peak-top. We stood in the wind. There was the high, pure sound of molecules humming in their vast spaces as they spin. They are voices, they are beings, actually angels turning through their paces, doing what they have been ordered to do, scientifically, with the purest order, strictly, in a geometrically flawless and rigorously exact formation.

Everywhere you look here there is perfection. Star shapes, radial spokes, unfoldings from a hinged interconnectedness, from tree-branch to lung, from dust-mote to star-crater, on one folding screen, folded up and leaned against a blank wall in an empty space.

There is no darkness, but there is no light either.

There is no sound, but no silence.

4th Day

Love here is not like anywhere else.
There is no equivalent anywhere else. *There* it was feeling
surrounded by body.
Here it is body surrounded by bliss.

The core of it burns with molecular passion
that has no hot wind in it,
no scorching emotion.

There such love could be hate in a moment.
Here it is stable, like breathing was formerly.
All around us, inside us, above and below us,
the object and subject of love is one touch.

There you could give it out, lonely in space.
Here there is no separation, one place,
one moment brings out all its delights.
Tree-twig and air that surrounds it

is one light.

5th Day

I'm losing my appetite for speech. Words of these kind are sucked
into a vacuum of pure light and a world of meaning closed to the
senses and any taint of analogy. It is pure and simple here, and there
is nothing like it.

An old man came towards me today, and as he came nearer I saw the landscape horizon of clouds behind him through his form as if it were a window washed clean. As he approached I saw that he was not old at all, but a radiant youth with all that first-fruit freshness of as yet unplucked awareness. When he was quite close to me I saw in his face the face of all the prophets, with our father Adam's first, that anthology golden original to all faces and forms that followed. And at the end, after all the prophets' faces had projected with a flickering and easing of features and a slow-motion explosion of eyes, eyes of such depth that whole skies could fill them and they could still hold more, at the end of that cavalcade, our beloved Prophet Muhammad, whose face is both sun and moon in a place that has seen neither, but only one Light. The man melted into my own form at last and walked away to the right, down a musk mountainside. I remained as well as departed. I was here as well as there.

There is less and less to say.

6th Day

Projected... transported... delivered... carried in the crops of green birds... escalated... lifted and projected forward... streaming forward toward a point... seen, unseen... behind me, before me... swept beyond even the movements of it... swelling... expanding... disappearing completely, yet watching... watching out of the air... seeing from nowhere...

dhat!

7th Day

(Diary ends here.)

THEY CAME DOWN

They came down from their various elevations.
They left it all behind. They had to.

They assembled on miles and miles of stretching
cloud or land, and it made some sad to

stand side by side by anonymous candidates
sinking in self-centered thoughts of the past.

Some sobbed emotionally, some stiff-lipped, silent,
some hoped to be first, others to be last.

Circuses circled in slow loops around mountains
unwinding all of humanity forward,

low moans and sharp laughter, echoes eternally
caught here in canyons where one single roared word

lit up the air in a sudden unveiling,
Allah's Name pronounced just once on the lips

in true recognition of His realm made visible,
now no doubts remain about making those slips

of forgetfulness leading one down a shale pass
to sink lost forever in a dark, thick mass,

nor any doubt about all those times of pure love
that fit the clear heart like a hand fits a glove.

Roadways now open, they stretch like light-beams,
open and radiate outward in timelessness,

all of the mirrors stand up on the desert,
their eyes searching far for the sign that will say *"Yes!"*

to let them surge forward, each one, one by one,
to the light that shines at the end of each tunnel

of each individual standing on actions
that poured their meaning to this place like a funnel

pours all the contents of a packet into a bowl,
or all the sand from one side of the hourglass

to reappear on the other, far side here
of existence's single one way pass.

Meanings stand up, their skeletons glimmer.
Their hands are making the gestures of each

single action ever done in the world,
here speeded up, to bear witness and teach.

The books appear, their pages are flying,
molecules turning slow-motion in space.

They whirl around bodies of each individual
and shine their writing on each one's face.

Some eyes pop like saucers, hair stands straight on end.

Some smile quite simply. No thing to defend.

Some faint in their place, screams lick their exteriors.
Some cast their eyes into brilliant interiors.

Some are led off to the Place of Long Groans.
Some stand transported in speeding light zones.

Stillness pervades here, it walks with slow strides
into openings opening inside and outside.

Arrived, no longer themselves, they are washed
in the river that flows without moving forward,

then in bodies like glass tubing, flexibly walk
on the bright green shore that starts moving toward

a place filled with emptiness, castles and palaces,
trees upside-down, crystal lakes, endless moonlight,

but all multiplicity here is reduced
to one optic chamber taking in just one sight,

and swiveling, rotating, circling, it takes off,
it flies without lifting, it lifts without brakes off

extending its width past whatever width sits here
at the edge of visually all that exists here.

The lover is brought out, his face is like water,
he walks to the edge of the lake and dives in.

He never stopped saying over and over
The One Name that made his own name grow thin

then one day pop altogether, no stray bits left
to say what was taken in Divinity's swift theft

that takes all at once, no evidence left back,
but moves it all forward on the one, single, true track

that's oiled with the grease of love, shining its essences,
pointing to vanishing points on far space-fences

fencing the end of all space from pure endlessness,
the step one takes walking right out of all "no" and "yes."

No opinions or actions are possible here,
they stay held in skeletal fixity for each year

stood up in their singular meaning emitting
electric signals to send signs transmitting

intentions clear as silhouettes set up
in front of the screen of first light, with no let-up.

They catch all the acts with their subtle nuances.
It is total replay with full consequences.

White dunes stretch out like soft cheeks or warm snow,
and deer in fine arc-patterns leap in one motion, slow

and ceaseless, disappearing, their hooves in the air.

Figments of light, slow, like sparks, sail everywhere.

For millions of eons in slow motion unrolls
the judgment on actions once done out-or-inside,

and each tiny moment, in full four dimensions,
displays now on big screens what each tried to once hide,

the ticks and inflections, the tones of voice, eye-rolls,
elegant camouflage, hyper-denial,

smallest kindnesses, warmths, recollections,
the one time you saw what was needed was one smile.

So, one to the Garden for lifting an insect,
one to the Fire for scowling in rage.

One to the Garden for looking the other way,
one to the Fire for shredding a page.

One to the Garden for seeing the Brilliant One,
one to the Fire for rotting in spite.

One to the Garden for once getting everyone
safely out past the edge of thick night.

One to the Fire for tricking the innocent,
one to the Garden for earning his pay.

One to the Fire for covering up what was meant,
one to the Garden for guiding the way.

Eyelashes wept on one man, so he went to green
shade upon shade under elm-boughs down-drooping.

Harsh throats continued to cry hoarsely negative
epithets in crazy thought-patterns looping

against the One Truth that, so evident, opens
the sky like a sky-ceiling wider than seas.

The Fire attracted moths to its flame-licks —
to the Garden swarmed citizens humming like bees.

A phantom bridge thin as a knife-blade first stretches
from near edge out to a cloud of far light.

The citizens now step out like quick sketches
to go to that place that lies just out of sight —

the bridge that extends its hair-length from the first world
past death to leap across canyons of Fire.

Each citizen had to cross all of its distance hurled
high with their purity, or slogging in mire,

whatever of good or bad actions they came with,
stepping off gingerly, the bridge firm beneath.

Some swept like a cyclone in one flash of wind, gone,
onto the far side with light from their teeth.

Some of the highest ones leapt like a lightning bolt,

only the back-flash of where they had been showed.

Enjoyment of bliss was their portion in each life,
they praised the Rain-Maker's mercy and flowed

like a flood to the banquet their destiny set out
on banks of original light, and no harsh shout

disturbs their feasting heartbeats and eyes,
and nothing in all the worlds comes as surprise.

Others on horses charged snorting across,
others like champion runners, their muscles flexed,

labored and sweated, but ran the full length of it,
centuries passing, their poor bodies vexed

by pumping and hard breathing, sweat like gold drops
pouring down skin that is new like fresh crops.

Others ran slowly, up hills on that knife-blade,
crawling to get to the top, out of breath.

On hands and knees, finally, panting and desperate,
each moment hitting them just like the first death.

Others were wobbly, teetering drunkenly,
finally unable to keep a fine balance —

fell off the sides to the Flame's fires licking
and jabbing with hot tongues as sharp as lances

the ones who had no way to keep themselves straight
on the bridge-edge that lengthens out farther than fate

to the opposite side.

The opposite side! The green bank! The shadows!
Rolling hills, musk underfoot, trees of shade!

Leafiest levels of thick shadows, pool-like,
cooling the citizens in soft green like jade

in the air, in the eyes, the skin green-tinted, tranquil —
water green, clouds greenish, words of peace, green —

all the cool scents and sweet smells of the chlorophyll
wilderness tinted each one with their sheen.

They roll on the hillsides and stand in the falls
that cup their water in pool reservoirs

of light upon light-waves eddying, lapping, erasing
all thoughts of the spiritual wars

fought on desert-flat, high-sea, mountain-peak, fortress,
to keep true worship from fading away

from hearts filled with darkness, the valve-locks of distress
loosened by what the sage Book has to say.

In an air of generalized celebration
and personal ecstasy held like a flare,

arc-lights leap in every direction
as weightless as air held up by air.

The Garden was planted with spirits like seeds
to gaze on the One Face forever, no veil!

Plants under sunbeams growing as plants grow,
sometimes cloud-bound, other times able to sail

freely roaming from light-spire to light,
motes in the air floating on, day and night

now unified totally, no *opposites* here,
They sail on forever, no time now, no year,

no moment, no lifetime puts chains on the neck.
Floating forever past worlds like shipwrecks

tilted and grounded on shoals of thick mud.
This place is all light that pours in full flood

without cease.

Without cease! The Name here is: *Endlessness.*
No beginning, no ending ever takes place.

It always was, present, it always was actively
contemplating His Generous Face

without motion or energy, matter or time.
The end is not marked by clock-tick or chime.

But one day it folds in a last expiration
and only His Face remains for the duration.

All time is no time. No space stretches out.
It all is resolved in Allah's Name.

Time — *out!*

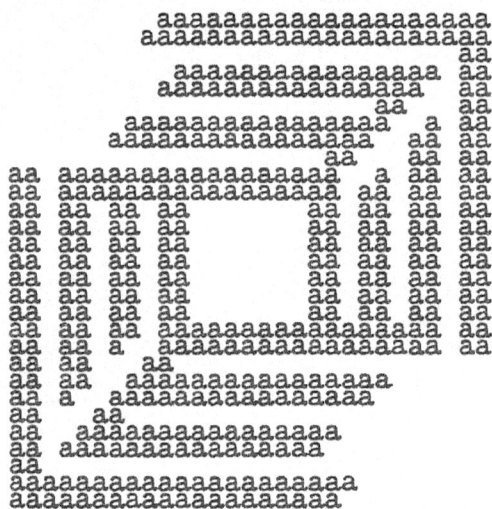

THE PERFECT MOON-FACED ONE

The perfect moon-faced one appears
with perfect lips and bow-like eyebrows.

His hair is braided behind his ears
and this pure appearance of his arouses

our trust that unity will thrive
and we'll be taken to One Presence

now that we find ourselves alive
in this world that is far less dense

than that of actions was before
when one thing made another happen —

here we find an open door
that there was only rarely open.

Praising, Praise, Praiseworthy, comes
hands raised at his sides, exalting,

takes us by our hearts and runs
through the various stations vaulting

past the barriers raised inside,
lusts and greed and deep reluctance,

knocks them with a touch aside,
keeps our steps firm with insistence,

leads us up no stairs to no height
but the one raised elevation

past the deepest realms of insight
to the Next World's happy station

face to face, our moon-faced one,
faces us past all formation,

praising that One with no space, sun
moon or stars, but all creation

gone in flashes no light shines on
to the last, uncluttered, single,

breath-stopped, stable, unique vision
in which all our gazes mingle

steady now, unchanging, direct
slow and slower eyesight finished,

just a mirror set to reflect
all the states, enlarged, diminished —

one breath streaming out past life
into worlds no eyes have seen.

There we find ourselves, no strife,
but one gaze that is evergreen

light upon a top-most tip

eye to eye, the "I" now gone —

emptiness, heart's deepest sip,
one gaze gazes on and on

NOTE ON THE TYPOGLIFS
by Karl Kempton, Illustrator

The Allah Series, dedicated to Abd al-Hayy Moore, is a segment of a book in progress, *Rune 7, Indian Wedding*. I am bringing together sacred visual expression from around the world and wedding it to like-minded expression of the Native American Peoples, primarily of the Southwest and Central Coast of California.

Page 14: *Bismillahi'r-Rahmani'r-Raheem / As-Salaam*: In the Name of Allah, The All-Merciful, The Most-Merciful / The Peace-Giver: Based on the general design layout of Southwest pottery. Op-box in center is made by the word *Allah* with the box representing the Ka'bah, the center point of Islam towards which the faithful bow five times a day.

Page 20: *La ilaha illa'Allah, Muhammadan Rasulullah* : There is no god, only Allah, and Muhammad is the Messenger of Allah: A combination of traditional Islamic calligraphic motifs which usually creates the silhouette of a mosque, but here also represents the Hopi altar.

Page 24: On the right, *Al-Muhyi*: The Life-Giver, and on the left, as mirror-image of itself, *Al-Mutakabbir*: The Majestic, two of the 99 Names of Allah, here representing Kachinas guarding the point of emergence, *Sipapu*, into the 4th world; each circle corresponds to one of the 4 worlds, the 4th being the top disk with the migration paths mapped out.

Page 27: *Allah, Muhammad, 'Ali* (God, Prophet, and devotee / caliph / shaykh) surrounded by Southwest designs of pueblo, sun, cloud, and arrow.

Page 29: *Allah*, based upon Navaho sand-painting design.

Page 34: *Allah*, made from the key of "a", our first letter, which stands for the beginning.

Page 39: *Allah*, with another *Allah* inside it, which implies endlessly unfolding gnosis of God.

Page 43: *Allah*, 8 representations of The Divine Name interwoven, one for each of the 8 directions, the 4 Cardinal points, plus upward and downward, inward and outward. Also a representation of the maze, the mystery we are born into.

Page 49: *Kun!*: Be!, the Creative Word surrounding The Divine name; maze pattern for Hopi migrations.

Page 56: *Kun!*: Be!, with rain design, rain for two desert peoples.

Page 63: *Al-hamdulillah!*: Praise be to Allah!: A circumnavigation of the Ka'bah by pilgrims, which says that Allah is the center of all things, and alone worthy of our praise and thanks.

Page 74: *Allah*: Based on the Indian swastica, a design made from the Little Dipper in its 4 Cardinal positions. This is a sacred symbol found wherever the Little Dipper can be seen.

ABOUT THE ILLUSTRATOR

Since 1974, Karl Kempton's visual poems have been nationally and internationally published in over 35 books, numerous national and international anthologies and magazines and e-magazines on the web, and exhibited in over 100 group shows. His work has evolved from typewriter to computer b&w to color and now mixed media with the aid of an SLR digital camera. Karl edited and published *Kaldron*, a journal of visual poetry, between 1976-1990 and is coeditor of an on-line edition published by Karl Young. He lives in Oceano, California with his wife, Ruth, growing micro-greens. She also teaches yoga.

MAULOOD

A poem in praise of
The Prophet Muhammad
peace and blessings of Allah
be upon him

1984

Hilye by Mohamed Zakariya

TRANSLATION OF THE HILYE
(by Mohamed Zakariya, Calligrapher)

Transmitted from Ali [son-in-law of the Prophet], may God be pleased with him, who, when asked to describe the Prophet, peace be upon him, would say: He was not too tall nor too short. He was medium sized. His hair was not short and curly, nor was it lank, but in between. His face was not narrow, nor was it fully round, but there was a roundness to it. His skin was white. His eyes were black. He had long eyelashes. He was big-boned and had wide shoulders. He had no body hair except in the middle of his chest. He had thick hands and feet. When he walked, he walked inclined, as if descending a slope. When he looked at someone, he looked at them in full face.

Between his shoulders was the seal of prophecy, the sign that he was the last of the prophets. He was the most generous-hearted of men, the most truthful of them in speech, the most mild-tempered of them, and the noblest of them in lineage. Whoever saw him unexpectedly was in awe of him. And whoever associated with him familiarly, loved him. Anyone who would describe him would say, "I never saw, before him or after him, the like of him." *Peace be upon him.*

Mohamed Zakariya, American Master Calligrapher (http://www.zakariya.net)

بسم الله الرحمن الرحيم

عن علي رضي الله عنه قال

كان إذا وصف النبي ﷺ ﷺ قال

لم يكن بالطويل الممغط ولا بالقصير المتردد وكان ربعة

من القوم ولم يكن بالجعد القطط ولا بالسبط كان

جعداً رجلاً ولم يكن بالمطهم ولا بالمكلثم وكان في الوجه

تدوير أبيض مشرباً دعج العينين أهدب الأشفار

جليل المشاش والكتد أجرد ذو مسربة شثن الكفين

والقدمين إذا مشى تقلع كأنما يمشي في صبب

وإذا التفت التفت جميعاً

وما أرسلناك إلا رحمة للعالمين

بين كتفيه خاتم النبوة وهو خاتم النبيين أجود الناس صدراً وأصدق

الناس لهجة وألينهم عريكة وأكرمهم عشرة من رآه بديهة هابه

ومن خالطه معرفة أحبه يقول ناعته لم أر قبله ولا بعده مثله ﷺ عليه

اللهم صلى وسلم على هذه الرحمة المهداة وشفيع الأمة يوم الجزاء وعلى آله وصحبه أجمعين

◆

And he who is guided to the blessed light, is well guided.
— Hassan ibn Thabit (d. 665 C.E.)

AUTHOR'S INTRODUCTION

The Arabic word "Maulood" (also spelled "*mauloud*" or "*mawlid*") actually refers to poetry or literature written in honor of the Prophet Muhammad's birth, peace and blessings of Allah be upon him, with all the love the Muslims have for him, and sometimes includes later events of his life known to all Muslims the world over. A mawlid, from the same Arabic root, specifically refers to the Prophet's birthday, celebrated in many parts of the Muslim world with joyously exalted devotional festivities which are frowned on in other parts of the Muslim world under the constraints of a more severe, even puritanical interpretation of Islam.

There is canonical precedent for mawlids during the lifetime of the Prophet, when Umar and the Prophet, may Allah bless them both, passed by a group of people celebrating the Prophet's birthday with song and the Prophet didn't forbid it, although some may dispute this tradition as weak. Legal opinions have been handed down by scholars to the effect that even if the mawlid is an innovation, it is a recommended one so long as the festivities include expressions of gratitude to God for the Prophet, and praiseworthy and positive celebration of him, peace be upon him.

This poem's obscurities and ambiguities may come from the fact that as I entered into it I found myself struggling with a western mindset to locate the Prophet Muhammad, peace and blessings of Allah be upon him, in our own cultural context, the western tradition, usually known as Judeo-Christian (seriously omitting one of its major influences: Islamic). And moreover a western tradition in which the Prophet, historically has been seen as a threat, as The Enemy par excellence, certainly to Christianity. This meant combatting the negative image of the Prophet from the Middle Ages on, appearing again almost daily or nightly in our late twentieth century (and now twenty-first century) news media. I was also searching for the lineaments of true prophethood and its meaning in American "cultural" patterning. The Christian idea of a prophet is Old Testament, and even a bit pejorative (wild men ranting about the end of the world, etc.) So the establishment of the honorable status of prophet is not a "given" in our society, who sees Jesus, peace be upon him, as a miracle-martyr Son of God, or as God Himself (for Muslims impossible), rather than as the human prophet-messenger of a spiritual teaching direct from God, and in that sense, bringing the same message as the Prophet Muhammad, peace be upon him: submission to Allah, to God — Islam.

If this isn't confusing enough, I must say that I was writing not for Muslims alone, for this was meant as a thematic not a ritual, or recitable, *Maulood*, but also for the souls of people embedded in a society that enshrines entertainers and sports stars over anyone with a known spiritual dimension. Since in America we are in the spiritual Dark Ages, literally, looking down on traditions other than our own whose notions of spirituality, even in a generalized and oversimplified way, often far outstrip our own, I found myself reaching for often outlandish "subconscious" imagery in order to get under the subject, the search for Muhammad, peace and blessings of Allah be upon him, in the American psyche. In Morocco it is enough to say "Beni Hashim" ("the tribe of Hashim," the Prophet's tribe) and people start to weep. In America it's Elvis Presley, Madonna, or Shaqil O'Neil, enlarged video personalities who may not even be real, much less serious role models for a person's spiritual path.

LETTER 50 of Shaykh Mawlay al'Arabi ad-Darqawi

By Allah, my brothers, I did not think that any of the people of knowledge, may Allah be pleased with them, would deny seeing the Prophet, may Allah bless him and grant him peace, while awake, until one day I met some of them at the Qarawiyyin Mosque. We spoke about it with them. They told me, "How can it be true that one can see him while awake when he, may Allah bless him and grant him peace, has been dead for 1200 years and more? It is possible to see him in a dream, since he said, may Allah bless him and grant him peace, 'Whoever sees me in a dream has truly seen me. Shaytan cannot take my likeness.'"

I told them, "Certainly he can only be seen when one is awake, when the meanings — or we might say the thoughts — have moved him from the world of forms to the world of spirits. He sees him there without any doubt, and he sees all of his loved ones." Then they were silent and did not speak. I said, "He can be seen in the world of spirits." After a moment, they said to me, "Tell us how that is." I told them, "You tell me — where is the world of spirits in respect to the world of forms?" They did not know what to say. I told them, "Where the world of form is, there is the world of spirits. Where the world of turbidity is, there is the world of purity. Where the world of kingdom (Mulk) is, there is the world of the Dominion (Malakut). Where the lower worlds are, there are the upper worlds, and there are all of the worlds. It is said that Allah has 18,000 worlds. Each world is like ours. This is in the Hilyatu'l-Awliya, may Allah be pleased with them!"

All is contained in man while he is not aware of it unless Allah takes charge of him. Then He covers his attribute with His attribute, and his quality with His quality. Allah — glory be to Him! has taken charge of many of His slaves and He still takes charge of them and will do so until their seal, may Allah be pleased with them... I said: "Seeing the Prophet, may Allah bless him and grant him peace, is not far from the one who holds to his Sunna and takes on his character. He is not disappointed and does not fall short. Good does not go far from him. This is my belief, and we will believe it until we meet our Lord.

From *The Darqawi Way*, translated by 'Aisha 'Abd ar-Rahman at-Tarjumana, Diwan Press, Norwich, England, 1979

(Note to the following poem: The phrase, *"Peace and blessings of Allah be upon him,"* is always repeated after the Prophet Muhammad's name, whenever mentioning him. Since the entire intention of this poem is contained in that phrase, and the actual repetition of it is not expected in panegyrical odes, please assume its presence when it is omitted, and that it is not omitted out of neglect or disrespect.)

STARTING FROM HERE

Starting from here
in order to find the heart that
    passes through station after station
on its way to the goal,

in order to see the flashing reflection in which,
against the whole starry background of the
    seen and unseen cosmos,
the light of the Illuminated One, Muhammad,
— beside whom there are only shadows —
shows,

no action needed,
no gesture of ours but the
whole rapidly fluttering celluloid motion-picture
threaded atomically through all the
    slits in the universe
at once
so that all scenes
at once
flash past
and are entirely resolved —

to see, to suddenly, with no guile, face
   to face, with no preconceived
cartoon however serious, no projected
experiential image, but rather

an image from himself alone beamed

outward to us from the innermost vantage

that the whole light burst forth
upon our shores in wave after wave of
pure resplendence, flowering flood after
   gush of foam in which each
      bubble is a picture and each
         picture inside is exact —

that the shine of the Sent One,
   Beloved Prophet Muhammad,
whose edges are
self's edges themselves,
edgeness itself, whose

total vastness is that in which we
sit or stand, by canyon's rim or
twilit grim protruberance
out like a peninsula into the oceans of the heart
   in terrestrial turbulance or
      sky's overturned
concave bowl of stars, all floating so lacily
   apart, held by fine webs of
      traceries finer than the
         finest thought of fineness,

that subtlest influence
that keeps things from snapping apart
and drifting off into alien spaces —

O Muhammad!

that face of his
bent from First Light
    over his hands in his lap,
under the Tree of Loyalty,

that being he was,
under the cloud that always
  shadowed him
      shading him —

that transmitter he was
of stature and nobility
to the creature of Reality
    most loved by God
but groveling in idolatry,

that Light that went ahead,
having been
the first Light shed
from the first burst
  from nothing but:

Be! And it is!

Being for us, having been from then,

the ultimate Word from the primordial Sea!

THE DIFFICULTY OF IT

The difficulty of it!

How to be so
  empty as to let
such pure praise
without the embroidery of personal snakes
    sing out!

Having gotten to here, poor human, so
caught up in the flow of traffic
  between the twin
rocks facing each other down the
trampled corridor of Safa and Marwah

constantly losing sight of Allah then hurriedly
gaining sight again, of that sharp sting,
that one essential thing in all our
    cycles, churning round and
      square and
round again, that aching
need to remember the One
unclothed with imagery.

To have gotten here, a dowser's wand, the
human hand, looking for wisdom's water,
    daughter of Time.

The bent shroud on legs who laughs and
smiles in the social charade,

but passes onto a platform of snow
to the train to Siberia two hundred below
   One True Zero.

The human landed on two feet but losing his balance.

The human so biologically syrupy in all his
elegant vinery, finery of green vines
so clenching around him, throughout him, in his
vein-vines and capillaries of penny arcade lights
   of acupuncture nerve-endings
      connecting him to the stars.

Poor human wreck, nothing salvaged but the ship's log
cataloging loss after loss
of his poor flesh in piles
   at the out-gate, exit ramp
      up to the dark wind in his face
as he goes without shoulders or lies
to the place of full light!

Getting here with all my sweats and grunts
   of humanity, like a donkey
      dreaming wings,
like a straw flashing by in a wintry wind
thinking to itself, *"I'm a promontory, a*
   continent, a galaxy on my
      way to the wheatfield's banquet
         at the edge of day!"

No sooner does it fall to the ground

but it blends with the rubbish around it,
blemishes and all, melting into
     the generalized patchwork.

How can the ignorant fisherman load his net with lies
and hope to catch real fish?

How does a pretend horseman
who's never been out of his chair
hope not to be thrown to the ground
  by the first real stallion he rides
     over bushes or through fire?

This is the poor human shivering from desire
to see and praise Muhammad, that noble one,
who threaded the thread of humanness
through the rare needle of how to
     worship the Real
with no weltering back, no
          ambiguity, each

dripping second ticking us by on a sure track.

He held the needle up for all to see

and with it sewed a cloak

for all to wear

comfortably.

SPECTACULAR BRIGADES

1

Spectacular brigades of centipede travelers
   set out at all hours
      along the clock of the white rose
in search of you, or your last known stopping place,
O Muhammad,

or the centrifuge that will locate your
shadow on the curlicue screen of subatomic particles
      etched for our enjoyable inspection.

Traces of what was
become traceries of the future
   we stand between
     awed
by the bubble-nature of what is.

Search-parties leave the side of the comfortable ostrich egg
to find you, and take up
   collapsible heros
in the social necessity of having
   someone who knows
      how to be
at the helm.

Empty sandals take the weight of any foot
   and make an imprint with it
leading up dubious Himalayas of a

long forgotten Utopian dream that
    won't come true.

The mists hang heavy
and the Chinese themselves may be having
  trouble realizing the Tao
against the clatter of populous conformity
   all buttoned up
     in their tight blue jackets.

Anything will do for most people,
a profile in snow
that melts at the drop of a light ray,
a torn photo album of the flashiest rock star,
the physiological gesture parade
    of poses and poseurs
who won't go away.

The cardboard tree of famous faces is enormous
and flowers anew at the start of each
      season.

But the naked heart, meanwhile, aches
and mortality's ashes are mounting.

2

A hero is not easy
  when his diaries are out
with their moisture of personal details

he hoped wouldn't show,

the haircuts, hair color, the way the body moves so
    among motorcycle savagery or the
        slick Garbo of night
    leaning back on a glass piano.

The molecule etchings leave
    leaf tracks in coils,

the whirlpool corkscrew sucks
    everyone down.

A yell on the desert won't squeeze
blood from rocks
who sit like lizards
in millennial silence.

A scratch on vinyl, on window or door,
like a voice trying to articulate
        that special humanity,
calls out by that gesture
    the final appeal
that can't go unheeded by the
heartache that speaks it.

There's an answer in the two-way mirror of the air
out the eon's volcano cone mouthpiece lying sideways.

It's an image of outline on a camel against the sun's
like a bloodburst coppery heat-saucer burning.

The caravan jangles its nerve-endings and decamps.
The horsemen get on and make the tongue-cluck
    that starts it.

There is a setting out. There is a
    footfall, a bloodbeat, a
pulse in the life cycle that moves out along a line.

There's a something that can't be denied when the
    umbilical is cut
from womb world to 3-D shock-absorber matter,
and what was swimming upside-down
    in an ocean of whale thought
comes out by the lamp of on-again off-again light,
and is turned around for all the waiting
      relatives to see.

There's a secret, a secret inside a secret,
and that secret inside a secret inside a secret is an
    ocean without shores

lapping for multiple forevers
in a single snap of nothingness

inside the newborn soon-to-die flesh heart beating

like a rabbit alone in snow
under an eagle's watchful eye.

Each life line stretches mysteriously

from before the Creation
where a fish-shape of mist
hangs on the end with round eyes staring.

It's a push, thrusting with head down, shoulders
    hunched forward,
  to get away at the same time as arriving
      like melting ice.

It's a swift throb from the ocean in the heart
    without shores
that laps for a single moment and like a
    trumpet-note goes on.

It goes on with its strident clarity
past a ring of forest beasts watching,
it goes on past the Andromeda Galaxy
with its spidery claw of light.

It carries the note-blower with it along the
    full length of its calling.

And this calling out in longing is the answer I've been
    seeking all along!

This rumble of knots that thumps on the
ocean floor of Impatience,

thrashing back and forth with the currents
    of births and hesitations.

3

One pointing finger set northward,
one keel set sail against breakers,
one true word that flies from lips with no
    ulterior motive,
  to see the window light up around

the face of the one who is in it.
Illumination of crushed sand atoms —

Muhammad, portrait of the creation
    entire
in one face!

Eyes almond ovals, eyebrows arching over
like lithe Arabian bows meeting in the middle,

nose long and finely chiseled,
face round and pale, truly moonlike,

lips meeting beautifully, beard-hairs
  long and lustrously black,

hair curly like sand-dune waves,
  dark and light in alternate shadings

oiled like the glistening sea that
stretches out its strands in the moonlight —

so it is moonlight on sea waves,

it is
this face that contains the cosmos, these

burning eyes with fierce purpose,
soft as a mother's, steady as a warrior's.

This light stands high on its camel.

This leader goes ahead of his flock.

This flock is ourselves.

MUHAMMAD'S BIRTH

About his birth the whole world knows
    in the depths of its atoms.

Amina bore him and he was immediate
    in his praise of Allah.

Some say he first did sajda, others
    that he spoke the shahada
      and then was silent.

Already at birth he was the Prophet of Unity, the
    movie played backwards
      from its glorious end.

His father Abdallah, from the tribe of Hashim,
    died without seeing him.

The wet nurse Halima took him to her heart
    and their goat's milk flowed.

All the desert burst into sumptuous flower
    from his singular presence.

The nighttime covered him
    with its spangled blanket.

The day fluffed the wool of its sides for him to
    tend it like huddled sheep.

A cloud went with him to shade him from the heat
    at the desert saint's surprise banquet.

(He could see the Prophet's space among the
    caravan leaders and
        called out for him to fill it —

"Where is the boy who has come, by Allah,
    to show me the Prophet's seal?" — a mole
it is said, between his shoulder blades, with
    circling hairs like a horse's mane.)

He grew up trustworthy among men for whom
    this was a difficult quality.

He took from the cloth of Unity
the Black Stone of Eternity

and placed it bodily
in the side of God's House,

cornerstone finality,

stone we kiss

out of awe of God's Majesty.

THERE WAS NO ONE LIKE HIM

To say there was no one like him
    is to say
there was no one like him!

God knows best about this
    but we say
"There was no one like him."

The best way to get even a tiny glimpse of who he was
is to recall some person with extraordinary qualities
who passed by in a moment
or stayed for a season, whose
  sweet nobility awed you, or whose
spontaneous depth of knowledge,
  taken out from some
    deepsea nets whose
  strings you couldn't see
    nor whose source fathom,
light after light,
load of richness,
  dredged from the deeps...

Or someone you loved whose every gesture was
  meaning, whose
    still center was a
camp of tents, in each tent a
  prince whose otherworldly
    beauty swept you away.

A snowbound romance
between two summers
whose heat melted it away
leaving only a positive memory and no
   sculptor's regret
not to have "caught it in stone," or to have
   kept it forever frozen.

Someone whose strength seemed to be
summoned from an ancient animal kingdom
against a violence of nature that flooded from nowhere,

or someone whose sudden sweetness surprised you
and made you want it to last your whole lifetime
   past the closing door down the hallway,
but who went on to a similar succession
      of such personal sweetnesses.

Or the Buddha, sitting crosswise to everything.

Or the linkage of radiances connecting its dots
   through the globe
 in discrete places, in out-of-the-way
     locations —
a generosity that saved someone from drowning
or a word that turned a life all the way around —

this, these, one after the other,
commonly continuous, all of them and more,

forming a whole man in this world where everyone is a

partial enigma jigsaw,

forming a clear focus in a
   dangerous fog,

a light standing up
   in a subway of shadows.

In a world gone galvinized tin,
   a sensitive liquid.

He was like no one.

The peaks of all possible humanness
   folded into one.

He had time for everything and everyone.

Nothing that exists kept him from
   anything else in existence.

He himself was an empty mirror, but
   the frame was the cosmos
     aflame in the dot

that sits below the letter *ba* in *Bismillah*
   — *in the Name of Allah*
and bathes everything in light.

This is no fiction.

His Companions
  like lenses
on the same occasion
  caught sight of him the same
and recorded identical conversation
  as multiple observers

so that a verbal movie of him exists, walking
  alone among them,
a world not gone in a burst
  once gone,
but alive forever on the transmitted
  heart screen of emptiness.

Gentle humility shook the earth's foundations
since true knowledge funneled in discs of exploding
  light through it.

Tattered poverty sent proud kings flying
since it endures after golden thrones have turned
  impossibly to dust.

Face down in the dust
the tyrant is wild-eyed.

He fears for his neck
as God's rose-thorn digs in.

But the Prophet's face down in the dust
pushed its light through the stars

spread out in an array

that will never go away.

There was no one like him.

NINETEEN-EIGHTY-FOUR

Are there other isolate men sounding out the alarm
on the midnight of 1984
as the world goes dead drunk
    around them?

It's not Big Brother who is watching
but the Face of the One Reality
Who has never
    taken His gaze away
  and recalls each detail.

No nightmare but the one we make
  3-D and populated
with pastel or neon recall
    down to the last detail.

No movie but the one we project
by our conscious greed involvement
in everyone else's business but our own
rather than the one at hand
    that really matters,
the recall of that Name, that divine detail,
  that opens the conch shell like a bolt,
      slow-motion coiling to center
    down to the last detail.

Down in the hole, the world itself
with its political hail-storms,
down in the heart itself when not covered

over with suits
    of another business but the
        business of the heart,

down in the dog-drift elegant shoot-down
    mire of mad drunk nightmare
        blaring its
    car horns in the traffic of metallic dream,
        that actually crushes the pedestrians
            and on waking

has left real corpses in pools of their own blood
on Nicaraguan jungle paths

or Lebanese main highways out of town
    or the town itself demolished
        and totally gone.

Down there, in that mud-hole, down there in that mire,
the clear Face of The One also shines

and His Eye is steady.

NOTHING SO SMALL AS NEUTRINO OR GRAVITINO

Nothing so small as neutrino or gravitino,
less than a tiny click in a space less than the
size of a mote
    or even the shadow of a mote,

nor so large as the largest galactic cluster
    of scattering debris,

nor the mass and tilted swirl of the whole
  universe milk it all swims in

fails to call out your name, Muhammad,
by the mere fact of its being.

For *"There is no god but Allah"* is the single
uttermost Essence untainted by any
    shadow or substance
  of atomic grime or even the
      slightest tick of the time-clock
        running down,

and *"Muhammad is the Messenger of Allah"*
is the creation from that first breath
  of spirit, that first
    clutch of light that
had breathed into it: *Be Muhammad!*

Starting the spin-out of oceanic matter, in

whirlpool bang that is
  inside-out still more slowly
 stretching to the limits of
        Limit itself,
out and out to the greatest height and depth and width
like the spindly Lote Tree of the furthest
   limit of matter
reaching to the ultimate branch-tip,
    root-tip, edge and lip of
silhouette latticework spider web nebula and wisp
of stars and starlight shooting through wave after wave of
        silent darkness
both alive and dead, both blue and red,

and behind that darkness, Black Holes or space pits
funneling matter and anti-matter into
     somewhere unknown,
   tight in its entrapment of radiance,
     Venus flytrap of light
   that lets none out —

nowhere, no side pocket,
lung, eye-socket, drain or
heartbeat

silence or shout

that does not call out
the syllables of your name:

Muhammad,

praised one,
existence's Messenger

from the One True Existent:

Allah.

TINY SPIDER ON A LEAF

The tiny spider on a leaf
knows you as he finds relief
from patient hunger winding spry
spider-silk around a fly.

The whale in all his deepsea booms
knows you as he moves through rooms
of sparkling coral lost in song
to a mile wide radius whale throng.

Worms in soil among the rocks
know you in their slimy clocks
of special worm metabolism
in cold earth's wintry hypnotism.

The eagle with his cloud-white plumage
knows you in his swoop and image
eagle-eyed of rabbit, crouched
in snow awaiting to be touched.

The dragonfly with nervous flutter
knows you as he sees the stutter
of his green reflection pass
across a pool's cool mirror mass.

The bear in polar ice cap winter
knows you curled in cave interior
as the season passes slow
around his sleep thirty below.

Seasons know you in their thaw
and flower, going suddenly raw
and fresh with green flesh ripe and new
and juicy in the morning dew.

The mite, the mote, mosquito, mole
all know you in their special hole
Allah has given every creature
to be its home and function teacher.

Drift in space of spray or light
know you by your face, ignite
the actions that so fill each speck
as matter sinks like a deepsea wreck.

Earth in all its daily rounds
knows you in its deepest sounds
of rising, falling, heaving, roll.
The earth's an ocean, sky its pole!

So every atom, lit, alone,
knows you from its nucleic throne
in isolation or in chorus
with all the atoms created for us

in every leaf or web or knot
or ripple of the stillest thought
across the pond of mind or pool
that stretches out its liquid jewel

like a net or radar cup to catch

the furthest spatial influence, thatch
of sound-waves crisscrossed with the flow
of particles in one long river glow

to make one glorious cry
to you, their Light, your gentle eye,
Muhammad, your presence in actual space
that put all meaning in its place,

for you preceded everything
that has dimension, casts a ring
of light or shadow around its head
of glass, or flesh, of vapor, lead

or creature, you were first, your dot
of light the one that flows in thought
to unite the streams of earth and sky
into one horizon in the heart's wide eye.

Muhammad, Messenger, your self-form
the pattern of all the living swarm
from thin to fat, from small to vast,
of all that flows between first and last

because Allah alone is First
and only Allah is Last, the thirst
for knowing Him must stop at that.
You are the City of Light's habitat!

MAN AMONG US

Muhammad whose genealogical tree went right straight back to Adam,
who said he was a prophet when Adam was between water and clay —
how can we properly praise him, surrounded as we are by madmen
who think they are sane and saviors, but who shrink from the light of day?

Muhammad, who at six was an orphan, and whose darkness was removed
    by angels,
who entered the valleys and date palms burst into fruit above him —
how can we possibly taste that quality of his wisdom
when oceans of plastic silence fill our ears with their deafening din?

Muhammad, who grew to be trustworthy, even his enemies trusted him,
who waited for three days on a corner to pay back a debt he owed
    someone —
how can such honor be followed, in a world so ethically stifled,
when the very foundations of trust have been laughed into mud and ruin?

Muhammad who stood on the mountaintop and saw the sky fill with
    angels
but distrusted such visions as raving and was afraid his mind had
    snapped —
how can we see such stillness in the pool of his heart so thunderstruck
when our own streets are hallucinations like savage animals trapped?

Muhammad who let the Truth lead him, and his moon-like light filled the
    tents
of the people whose hearts were empty but open as sky,
how can our people be touched by the stature of such a being
when most of them are full of sickness and most of them want to die?

Muhammad whose talk was like mountain streams clearly crossing
    rocks
and splashing into pools of clarity where we could finally see our
    light —
how can this thick time know him? The doorways are filled with
    ghosts,
the dumb are leading the eloquent, the leaders are fearful of insight.

Muhammad who went through the heavens on the back of the
    lightningbolt mule
and whose gaze was steady and true face to face with the Face of the
    One —
how can mechanical thinking or the heart like a clockface in ice
begin to glimpse this other world with its other moon and sun?

Muhammad who led the armies with nothing but banners and trust
against mercantile idol-subscribers with the weapons and wealth of
    kings —
how can simplicity make sense to us, so overpowered by the magic
of High Technology's sorcery which clots up our senses with "things?"

Muhammad whose victory just humbled him more than he was
    before
so that thousands finally accepted the worship of Allah alone —
is it the same situation now as then for us, hard-hearted people asleep
who'd rather sit in a stupor and worship bits of wood or stone?

Muhammad whose Gate-Opening crashed the iceburg rock right
    open
to let us enter a world where actual events shed light,
how to sit or go through a doorway, drink water or lie down to sleep,

how to face absolute Oneness without losing balance from fright.

Muhammad, peace of Allah be upon you, Prophet and Messenger of
    Light,
the figure you made among people put love in their hearts for the
    Truth —
how can the graveyard society we live in possibly hear your heartbeat
when their drunken hearts drink darkness sold at the tyrant's corner
    booth?

O Prophet, O man among us, O light that goes ahead,
who gave out the last coin left to you when you lay on your first
    deathbed —
how can such stark reality reach into us when the air is so filled with lead
and such mention of life only bores the snoring multitudes of the dead?

O Light of the human touch in everything, Praiser and Praiseworthy in one,
we are naked before Allah at last, and we need your enlightening sun!

YOUR EYE WAS STEADY

Your eye was steady
and no one but Allah knows how many tears you shed
or how many visions displayed their
details to you as you sat or stood
by any tree or shadow of a tree
in this place.

Your words were clear
and everyone could follow them
like pearls on a string,
each one individually strung
and each one lustrous enough
to reflect Allah's Face.

Your gestures were simple,
a raised hand or a lowered hand,
a raised eyebrow or smile
that was enough to move
multitudes of ant-like scrambling
and bring some breath of tranquility
to this ant race.

Your guidance was pure
and you left the teaching complete
to the uttermost detail or
indicated dimension of detail,
all of it filled with the Light of Allah
and your own self gone
with no trace.

Your created the sound hearts of men
by the raising up or lowering
of those who were too held down
or too proud and who
came into your shimmering dimension
treading the creation with
a shooting star's pace.

We yearn to meet you
face to face by the side of the
bowl of sweet nectar in the Next World you will
pour out for us cup by cup
to slake our thirst and
wash out the last dark shadows
from our Original Face.

In this world you were perfect,
in the next you are light
that takes our cracked souls
from their darkness and places them
face to face with the

Owner of all Praise!

THE BEE AND THE PEACOCK

1

How could the bee know her way through the
dazzling turnpikes of the air straight to that
   delectable signal in the flower's core?

How could she dance the code of gyroscopic
accuracy, fittingly harmonizing with the
molecular jitterbug that vibrates everywhere
     accordingly?

How could she come back so loaded
with pollen-boots heavier on her
   spindly legs than Inuit mukluks,
hiking back to the center where
perfect geometry takes over, elegant
hexagons in the bee's loud refinery?

The Qur'an says
the bees are inspired, that
God inspires them to build
   houses in the hills and under eaves
and to manufacture a curative liquor,
   so that
things are set straight for them,
wheels set in motion, they
know what to do on this earth

forevermore.

They browse among furry lips of languorous lilies,
they slide down in and do their
elemental sipping. They zoom
without distraction,
making a bee line to where God has
placed, in various biological pots,
    the nectar and the knowledge.

We drink their offering, the juicy
product of their gathering,
alchemized from golden dust
to a medicine of many colors,
whose properties, like milk, cure

    many a malignant humor,

and it is said if you die with honey inside you,
    recently sipped,
you go directly to the Garden,

for like attracts like in
 the whole kaleidoscope of creation,
   and the spirit shoots like an arrow
to that which it was and to
that which was found inside it.

The eaves are dripping with honey drops
around the ears of our waiting here,
and honey-drips from the faucet of patience to be
    alone in the night
remind us of that

place we go to for spiritual freshness
the way anger goes to a
    fist and dilated capillaries,

or sweetness sits in the lair of the
        heart

like a lion looking out.

2

How can the creation be so filled
with appropriate exactness?

Precision to be what it is, doing what it does?

The arch leaps over into extraterrestrial territories,
but the shadows on the wall
    are precisely the same.

Everywhere you look in the universe
you see the same thing.

The same matter unfolds itself and folds up again
redefining its emptiness, re-displaying its

    O its peacock
white fireworks fanning
    tails of *tajalli* epiphanies!

Those
shot bursts of manifestation
   splashing outward simultaneously
in all the revolving mirrors of space
      at once!

No where is the same.
And nowhere is different.

The sea slides by
 on its oily rollers

across fragments of the whole

bobbing freely in their place!

BY OUR SMALLNESS WE KNOW YOUR VASTNESS

O Prophet of Allah, by our smallness we know your vastness,

by our electron microscopes we know in this world
how very little of the whole world we can know —

what shape we are in, what velocity through space, how
    organically we are connected
to everyone else in this race that has
  spread out so thoroughly from the
        loins of Adam.

Right now, our knowing ourselves to be alive,
that sense of total infusion between sound of
    motorcycle on the street outside
with the picture of silver-edged sublimity we have of you
superimposed in out-of-time dimensions
for the gesture of transmission to be triggered
1400 years ago through the tumult of time
        to now!

Transparency of leaf over leaf
in the leaf mold of totality!

Layered celluloid maneuvers of still pictures
    to the illusion of motion.

Has time elapsed since the first time
    Allah blew into His
      Light and said:

Be Muhammad?

Has the fish embryo developed into rapacious shark
with slit eyes and merciless teeth
   who turns its white bulk
     and swims away?

The sands of Sayyedina Muhammad stretch in all
six directions at once!

Connecting us to that first sand grain
    puffed into space
that finds its place in the sea of a trillion grains
one so next to the other
or so on top of the other, or so underneath

in infinite array past
all mathematics but the supra-elemental
   accountancy
that goes on to a zero
that drops its silver egg
into the infinitesimal yawn of space
  who feels nothing
    and goes on as usual

since nothing at all has happened
but the repetition of the Divine Name
  on Its Own Lips

in the everywhere at once of original night.

O Prophet of Allah,
you were sent out of this

to tell us, being of it, to lead us, being
from it, to its

Source, its spark, its

original
one time

special
stopping place.

RARE JEWEL

The rare jewel is carried in to the drawing room
and the royal face explodes with surprise.
Never has such otherworldly dazzle
so filled the vision of human flesh eyes.

The farmer looks out on his cornfield
and each ear is diamonded with dew.
An angel is standing on each tassel
wrapped in horizons of silver and blue.

A stag's head appears in the forest
exactly as in the brave's vision dream.
For a moment he stares at the dream beast
and they are linked by a single time beam.

The explorer reaches the North Pole
and expanses of white nothing stretch out,
but in his heart he knows he's hit center
and in his bones he hears an iceberg-deep shout.

The unjustly imprisoned prisoner
feels the men at his back fade away
as he runs through the now open fields
and escapes in the light of day.

Each is a moment of lightning in slow-motion,
of earthquake too interior to see,
of death of the norm in an eyeblink
and going on in a new world whose tree

of crystal lights shoots out through dimensions
with roots upturned in the sky
and branches down in the darkness
of the earth's musky moist blind eye

so that roots take light from Elsewhere
whose Light ignites hearts without cease
along lines of transmission from Source
whose electricity is fathomless peace.

THE MIND SHOOTS DOWN CORRIDORS

The mind shoots down corridors
  guided by an echo
    toward that dazzle of light
spray of eagle-flight opening out valleys
      entirely four-dimensional through which

one lone man in long robe and turban walks
on his way to the Ka'ba.

The heart looks directly into itself without hindrance,
  smoke past, light gone, air extinct,
senses closed up with various corks of darkness,

and no-place is any more than anywhere else
not that place of direct sipping,
the long drink
  from the longest Source,
    flash as a bright dot
      flat as a sphere so hot
  it sizzles down through icy atmospheres
    outwardly transpiercing no particular
      where in all directions
to here!

Sight longs to journey to the Prophet's bright side
and sit in his shade and drink in his light.

Cut away towering highrises, slash through
  escalating nations and

proliferating crates of what is eternally useless,
   the car-doors of enmity slammed
      shut and shooting down
         freeways to the Fire
that awaits all unsmelted metals at last
in the crucible of purity!

Tons of debris topple eternally into that blaze!

But what animates our days is the
   breath-span to reach to where
      wisdom makes its
     clarified cutting-edge in the
        commonest air,
that springs out its elegant cherry blossoms in
   the animate air, that
     is triggered by the Prophet's figure of
uncomplicated behavior, a sprig
       so light it is
     balanced on nowhere!

To see the whole history of those
foot treads, those smiles where his teeth flashed, the
lifting or lowering of his hands at his side,
the lifting or lowering of his eyes
by which men knew whether to build up
     or tear down in the
collapsible earth that is always, animated by the
        circuitry of the Decree,
reaching its pure ultimate conclusions and then
    dissolving at the same time into the

outbreath of a higher frequency —
　　blood rate tadpole
immediately becoming a frog
　　　and hopping away!

To see that one our essence so loves, that
kiss of atoms whirling essentially alone
in a lover's vistaless paradigm
lost on an edge somewhere and hopelessly
　　hoping to fall
　　　　off!

To go on, to go past it, to go up to it
then right through it,
sword of Elegant Certainty
angled through the bulk of each
　　dark cloud,
to the place of his residence
　which is in no
　　　corridor of air
the mind goes down
guided by an echo
　　toward that
　　　　dazzle of light
spray of eagle-flight opening out valleys
　entirely four-dimensional through which

one lone man in long robe and turban walks

on his way to the Ka'ba.

ADAMIC MAN

Adamic Man!
 The complete pattern for
  territorial cockatoo flight
   peninsula and heavenly
 birthright dimension to be
  the lone open human alive
   on this promontory!

Calling us back to that height!

The loud and subtle
 throb in us to go there
  by whatever shy darkness or sly
   light we have, burrow
into our selves past the
  blight of tomorrow
    to that
      spot!

He was the pattern and the meaning, the
outermost edge of being
and the innermost outflow
  of so much
    wisdom imprinted in the

  chains of the air!

THE TRUTH AND THE LIE

The Prophet walked alone in long robe and turban
on his way to the Ka'ba

and his enemies strewed spiky thorns
on the path for him to tred on

in the pre-dawn dark.

Truth walks among snares.

He prostrated at the Ka'ba
and when his back was arched

his enemies draped slimy animal guts
across his neck while his

forehead touched the ground.

The Lie displays its wares.

LIGHT OF THE SHADOWLESS ONE

When an object casts no shadow, what does it mean?
That its light is over all other lights
      and no light can
      come from any direction
and be stronger, cutting silhouette
outlines of form and laying them out
      on a ground into which
         all forms must go at last?
But Muhammad was such a one.
They said
he cast no shadow.

O Muhammad!
How can we find you here among the ruins?
How can we see you?

The catalog of his attributes can start from
      anywhere and continue forever...
the way he parted his hair, the way he
      greeted the poor and fed them.
He once filled a valley between two mountains with
      the sheep of God's bounty, until a
hardhearted bedouin who could only see sheep
had the eyes of his greed put out by the
      dazzle of such generosity,
         and he turned from
being greedy for world to being
            ecstatic affirmer of God
      carried away on the backs of fleece

soft as the hair of angels.

O Muhammad!
How can we find you here among the ruins?
How can we see you?

One man, longing to see you, nearly fell out of a date palm
    when he heard you had come.
He had gone from teacher to teacher, each one
        telling of your impending arrival.
Sweet date meat of a man, the lightningbolt of your
            presence struck
    and threw him down while collecting dates,
for his longing by then
        had matured the meat of his
            innermost sweetness, and his
                pure heart
                saw you at once!

O Muhammad!
How can we find you here among the ruins?
How can we see you?

Or is it that we're not in ruins enough?
Is it that our fortified walls
    have not yet toppled down?
That the glass we erect to see through and think
        is so limpidly clear
is in fact
the opaque screen of our selves set up
for the magic lantern to throw its image on

with an illusion of movement and
    the assumption of purest transparency?
But are we still too coarse, too thick, not
    subtle enough in this
  haggard age with its tapeloop rumors of
      war?
The absolute nuclear outbreath
that deflates the entire material
  system down to the last
    particle, even this still
too dense, too
    cartoon to contain
  the spiritual emptiness needed in us to let
     your pure Muhammadan
      nature show clear?

O Muhammad!
How can we find you here among the ruins?
How can we see you?

The maddest love for the biggest diamond
is nothing compared to the
  love your companions had for you —
they saw your truth was true,
your step sure, your word an opening into
    God's domain,
and one man spat out the grapes he was eating
and took the sword you offered
  when he heard you say
that whoever took it and plied it (in *true* Jihad)
    until he was killed in the way of Allah

would gain the Gates of the Garden, and enter it —
no doubt troubled him, no shadow cast
    from your presence, only light —
so what is this
heartbeat one thousand four hundred years later
full of love for you
  by people who never saw you
    walking like a shadowless
      mountain among them?

O Muhammad!
How can we find you here among the ruins?
How can we see you?

Your compassion for an ant trail, a thief, a wretched man
with one piece of rope in his household
  and no other possession!
Take that rope, you said, and gather firewood which you can
    tie with that rope
and sell it in the market. Then with the
money you earn buy more rope which means you can make
  more bundles of firewood
    and be on the increase, O always be on the
      increase! —
the flow of creation which goes with the flow of
  galactic billowing, opening its
    giant petalled corolla
  through eternal darkness,
    our galaxy itself floating through space
      like a flower opening,
        constantly on the

increase.

O Muhammad!
How can we find you here among the ruins?
How can we see you?

Our galaxy opens its rose-like corolla of light
out through endless darkness,

and sight itself is
stunned when it

sights your sun.

O Light of Muhammad,
O shadowless one!

GLIMPSE

The best way to get even a glimpse of who he was,

not anyone we've known, but the sum,
not human attributes alone, but the

almost impossible memory of that one we've
never seen, nor caught in passing, nor dreamt,

whose reality is other than the presupposed expectations of
a perfect human being, simpler as well as more profound,

whose acts and responses spring from the Source
which is *our* Source, for what is

recognizable in him is in the genetic
horizon of our selves,

we are, of him, a part —
as he said,

"The true dream is a 27th part of prophecy,"
so how could we move in it, then, and not know him?

How, down to the single collective chamber of the
human heart, from which our

humanity springs?

That bending we feel

to what is sweet,

that dis-enclouding we undertake
to what is true,

that pilgrimage we make
to what lies at the center

of our own rough terrain,

of the completed life, at last, on the bed of our
last breath, of the entire world itself

at last
in the Mecca of recognition,

the exact spot where Adam stepped down
to begin on earth

stretching out along the whole span
to the last man.

Face down in the dust
the tyrant is wild-eyed.

He fears for his neck
as God's rose-thorn digs in.

But the Prophet's face down in the dust
pushed its light through the stars,

spread out in an array
that will never go away.

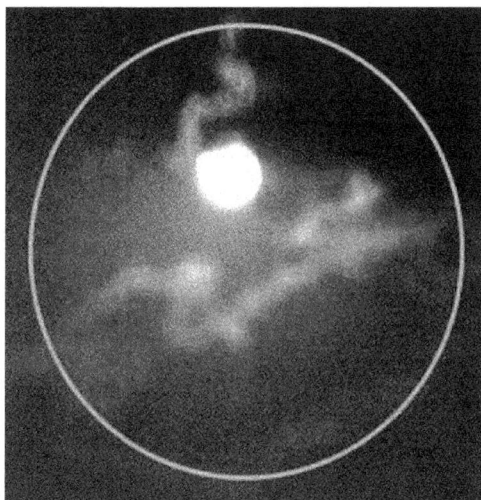

(Calligraphy of the Prophet's name in clouds, seen at a Celebration — Mawlid un-Nabi — in Lahore, Pakistan, 2007, "while Shaykh Muhammad Tahir ul-Qadri was elaborating on the name Muhammad, peace be upon him.")

■

MECCA/MEDINA TIMEWARP

December 18, 1995 — January 6, 1996

AUTHOR'S INTRODUCTION

These poems were written in Medina and Mecca during an 'Umra (lesser pilgrimage) performed at the end of 1995 and the beginning of 1996. Many of them were written in the Haram in Mecca, sitting among people contemplating the Ka'ba, engaged in remembrance of Allah, reading the Qur'an — recalling the many great people of Allah who have frequented the House of Allah, studied, written treatises, hoping that by taking my little notebook and my pen out of my bag, some of their scent might still be hanging in the air available for use, if Allah so willed.

For Muslims, the visit to the Ka'ba, whether on 'Umra or on Hajj, is the pinnacle of our spiritual life, a journey longed for always, the fulfillment of which is actually not expressible in words. In thinking about writing poems there, I wondered if I would need to employ completely surreal metaphors of the experience, mirrors set at oblique angles, as it were, to try to reflect some of the light less directly. Some of these poems partake of that approach somewhat, others are simply narrative word pictures, but none of them really conveys a presence that is so overpowering that when one first glances at the mosque from a distance, or enters it and sees the Ka'ba for the first time, a gush of tears pours forth involuntarily, the relief of all our mortal days, grief for our puny selves, joy at finally arriving at such a holy place, gratitude, awe, a combination so deep and so subtle that really there is no way to analyze it even if one wanted to. It is truly Allah's affair alone.

The Mosque of the Prophet Muhammad in Medina, peace and blessings of Allah be upon him, which is where he is buried, is a place of such sweetness and peacefulness and humanness that one of the greatest virtues one sees there is patience, serenity, and an overwhelming love for the Prophet, peace be upon him. It is a foregone conclusion that we are all there out of love for him, and with a longing for an increase in that love. So one feels an enormous brotherhood (and sisterhood) with people of all countries and races who are there with the same thing in their hearts. The Ka'ba in Mecca, on the other hand, is the place for a passionate outpouring of one's soul to Allah, directly, unmitigated by the usual niceties of human behavior, in the sense that holding onto the threshold of the door to the Ka'ba and weeping openly and calling out the most heartfelt prayers is in no way accompanied by a sense of embarrassment or shame; on the contrary, one may feel some disappointment if one isn't able to turn oneself inside out with sincere openness before God at this place. At the same time, this is a place of ennoblement of the spirit, where one's deepest humanness is most affirmed, in the most profound privacy on earth in a public place where cosmic openness is so apparent that one's heart is laid bare among the thousands, or even millions, of pilgrims who gather there.

I haven't approached the poetic expression of the experience here with any degree of calculation; I haven't consciously tried to encapsulate the ritual of the 'Umra itself, nor every aspect of our visit to both Medina and Mecca, including a journey to the sites of the Hajj, such as Mount 'Arafat, or the visit I made to Baqi, the graveyard just outside the Prophet's Mosque in Medina — where many of his wives are buried, his daughter Fatima, the Caliph 'Uthman, Imam Malik, may Allah be pleased with all of them, and even a member of our own modern community of Muslims in America, who went to Hajj and died in Medina a few years ago, and now is buried in such illustrious company, only a few hundred yards away from the Prophet himself. The contemplation of this fact even now puts shivers up my spine, since it is such an enviable place to be on the Day of

Resurrection, near to our Prophet, who will intercede for us with Allah at that time, among his Companions and wives, in the City of Light.

I feel the paltriness of these poems with some regret, and may have to wait for the true import of the journey to be transmitted to me and then somehow turned into poetry. In the meantime, as a kind of artistic journal, alluding to the inner meanings I experienced only indirectly, I offer them both to Muslims and non-Muslims for whatever savor they may have. I will say, however, that on the airplane back from Jeddah to New York, it struck me very strongly that from the time of the actual 'Umra ritual onward, for about nine days total, I had not had any extraneous thoughts! Everything had a kind of tranquil intensity, and although I did think, chatted, ate and slept as usual, our days and nights were completely dedicated to going to the Ka'ba to do *tawaf* (the seven ritual circuits around the House, reciting prayers and invocations), or performing the prescribed prayers with the congregation (never less than a few thousand, even in the middle of the night), and everything was somehow straightforward and clear. Just by being there, where the Prophet Muhammad was born, where Islam began, where many prophets are buried (under the marble slabs), where so many saints have come, have sat, have even taught, one is perforce in a state of remembrance of Allah, mindful of inner things, sensitive to a high degree to the moment, and the signs Allah might send in any one of them, and full of love for one's mortal companions, since the vision alone of the House of Allah is a vision of death, a vision of how insignificant we are, but more importantly, how overpoweringly significant God is. And there is no power and no strength but with Allah, the High, the Great.

Philadelphia, 1/13/96

"Know, my noble friend and intimate companion, that after I arrived in the Mecca of Benedictions, the Treasury of spiritual tranquilities and movements, and after I experienced there what I experienced, there came a time when I happened to be performing the ritual circuits around the Ancient Temple. As I was carrying out the circumambulations and reciting the formulas of glorification, praise, magnification and Oneness — now kissing the Black Rock, now touching the Yemenite Corner, now drawing near to the Wall of Multazam — as I was standing in a state of ecstasy in front of the Black Rock I encountered the Evanescent Youth, the Silent Speaker, He who is neither alive nor dead, the Simple Composite, He who envelops and is enveloped. When I saw him perform the ritual circuits around the Temple, like a living person revolving round a person who has died, I recognized his true reality and his metaphorical form, and I understood that the circuit round the Temple is like the prayer over a corpse."

— Shaykh al-Akbar 'Ibn al-'Arabi

A mouse is miracle enough to stagger a quintillion of infidels.
—- Walt Whitman

THE MIRACLE OF THE FOOT

The human foot is a consummate miracle.
It is not a horse's foot, cloven and horny,
it is not the clawed & scaly foot of the disappeared
    dodo,
it is not the first foot of earth dug out of the
     ground for our grave,
it is the human foot created in the perfect godly
  form of a foot, unique,

lovely individual toes articulated like puppets with
    soft underpads and protecting
nails on top. The little toe like Bo-Peep among

larger siblings, tender-hearted, frail.

The heel a sturdy tool for digging into
   sand, as Gabriel's heel was said to
strike the earth three times and the
miraculous waters of Zam-zam gushed out,

the ankle too like bony shields on either
side, facing laterally from the body's
forward direction, hub-caps in full motion,

which takes me to the true miracle, the
    greatest miracle of all,

that while the foot, and its partner the
second of a pair, is free, free to

walk where it will, with its
   tendons and complicated
musculature and bone structure,
free to take its owner
anywhere on earth,
and the whole human creature, self-propelled,
    is free to pick and choose and
go where it wants, trip the
   light fantastic, run the 100 meter dash,
     shuffle off to Buffalo,
tread a precarious balance over
   Dantesque crater-rims of Hell,

these feet, one foot at a time, one
   in front of the other, can
also carry their owners to Mecca,
walk the remaining steps under the
arches to the Great Mosque, stand facing the Ka'ba,
support the standing
pilgrim whose whole being has just

vaporized from head
to tingling toes

before

the greater

Presence of Allah.

12/18

MIRACLE OF THE DELAYED PLANE FLIGHT

Ants in a capped bottle can't get out.
Snow and ice and a broken windshield
   keep the Saudi Air jumbo jet
      from flying.
Like a giant moth with watersoaked wings
the airplane sits in the snow
muffled and downed.

Yearning pilgrims, asleep in airport chairs, gazing out the
      window at the wounded moth,
remembering God between bouts of heartbreak,
wait for the ban to lift, and themselves,
      into the sky.

Wait for the bottle to be uncapped and overturned.

Wait for the ants to remember the light of their
   destination in each footfall of the
      way.

We could be transported in an eyeblink
from Kennedy airport terminal with its
   disgusting bathroom facilities
to the sweet roar of bare human feet
whispering around the
House of God on clean marble slabs.

The snow falls
and the moth looks more forlorn.

The Ka'ba remains,
four walls and a door,
for us to surround.

The sound in the heart of the
heart's true murmuring.

LATER FROM THE NEW YORK HOTEL ROOM

Horn blasts from twenty floors down
aren't from ants who've been freed!

12/20

FIFTEEN HOUR FLIGHT TO JEDDAH

If you took the airplane out from
    under us for a moment
there'd be about three hundred people being propelled
    forward through space with
      sleepy or expectant faces,

each person's life would be perfectly
encapsuled in a gesture, light all around it,
space all around all of us on our
    way to Mecca — hearts like
      rose gardens trying to bloom into
flower in the middle of winter, green petals,
    blue blossoms, purple and scarlet
      buds popping out of
wiry stems — each person in space
a complete world, a history unscrolled in
      millions of static pictures,

each person in space right now
holding onto one or two pictures more
    cherished than all the rest,
zebras bounding through tall grass, the
    door of a white mansion opening,
the predictable dialog with siblings, a father's
      tubercular cough,
    echoing calls in the
night as from distant
    lone wolves on a
      lunar mountaintop...

Somehow with the material plane gone from
    around us, heading north-east,
sitting upright or hunting for comfortable positions,
the sky whizzing past us, a few
    stars visible, a sea of clouds or
        utter blackness,

the magnifying glass of God's compassionate focus on our
hearts becomes even stronger,

our mortal being broods over its faults and frailties,

tiny movements buzz from visceral hive to hive like
glints from furtive facets in crystal
somewhere deep in something we apprehend as
deep inside us — although boundaries
    evanesce at a moment's notice,
things inside slip with their symbolic resonance
suddenly outside us, outside recognitions
    spark elegant
        emblems
        within invisible pantheons —

zooming forward in space, nothing around us but
    space,

our feet end in five toes each
    making ten,

our heartbeats count their way to the
    Day of Doom,

each of our hair follicles shimmers unseen,

our eyes see or do not see

by Allah's Light.

12/22

SPARROW ON THE PROPHET'S TOMB

1

O sparrow perched on a corner of the
    Prophet's tomb
cheeping above thousands of bowed heads murmuring,
whose glassy chirps hit high notes of
    purity under the eaves in this
        Mosque of God's Messenger
that resides in two territories of space —
    this world seen, the next world
        unseen —

in this shadow existence of his signal presence among us
    visitors from even farther away than
        China pass by to greet him,
and in your little feathered body is the swooping freedom to
    come and go all day to visit him
speeding from a tall beam
    across choruses of hearts
gratefully weeping or tranquil with an ecstatic
        inner moonrise

just to be here.

2

Sparrow, what is your name? Is it *"Constant Devotion?"*
Is it *"I Want To Be Near?"* *"Praiseworthy Friend?"*

Is your name *"Generations To Come?"*
You fluff your breast and preen your wing
where men cannot go, you dart into the
dark of the tomb for deeper conversation.

We would all go with you if we could,
squeeze our tiny feathery bodies through the
   gold grille work, past the
      guards in their pea green uniforms,
to sit on a corner of the Prophet's tomb in the
   dark to hear him
return the salutations of
such outpouring awed adorations of men and women,
      each one
passing by that undying presence, trying to
sneak a peak through the golden porthole,
hearts boiling with overwhelming emotions.

You land and sing.
You cock your head.
You watch us from your high perch with a
      cool eye.

3

Sparrow, you are more than a sparrow.
You are a continent of sparrows.
You are The Minister of Internal Affairs of all
      sparrows.
You are the song that laces the margins of the deep message,

the message of God's Magnificence, the
thunder of tremendous shock, earthquake and
    heaven crash of the
stark glare of God's Might.

You trill and fly,
your song like a tiny tune from paradise,
    delicate celesta of celestial light.

The mosque in Medina expands
    all the way to the
        ends of the earth.
Forget about walls, where
marble pillars mark
the mosque's original dimensions,
the Prophet's precincts now
    encompass our houses and the
  invisible courtyards of our
        love, interconnected by

sparrow-song, perched on a
    Turkish cornice,

singing to Timbouctou,
Medina song bird

    heard around the
        world.

12/25

MECCAN SNAPSHOT

Any moment in time is the
  defining moment in time
in which a flash immortalizes our
  frizzle of electric life
from the marrow of our bones out
to the defining actions of our hearts.

Captured in freeze frame for all time.

The emblem that tumbles into our graves.

The calling out to our Lord like
  abandoned children
to keep us deeply connected.

These people
walking around the House of Allah with
various thoughts and faces, my
  various thoughts and faces
at this precise moment,

fear, desire, longing, light upon light
  expressing itself in our
    souls without cease,

around and around
in sublime perfection.

12/26

MIRACLE OF SOUND AT THE KA'BA

What sounds are heard around God's House?
First, utter silence, silence within silence. Then
      its echo,
         more silent still.

A silence that sits deep under the Throne of God —
all other silence surrounds it and
      slowly turns.

Every other silence partakes of that silence. Silence in
      eyes, silence in tongues, silence in the
womb, the silence of death.

The Ka'ba sits in the
shaft of that silence from the height of heaven,
and generates silence.

Then, just around this great circle of silence
the sound of an ocean, not of water or salt,
but of human longing, aswirl with
      sound, slow roar, slow-motion crash of
         surf, suspended animation of all
tremendous sounds in creation, the
exhalation of giant beasts, outbreath of
earth as God created caves and
      sea depths and

seismic shifts.

Then more distinctly,
articulating what shines through both
    silence and sound,
the Word of God,
that aural text that floats from the
Heart of Light into the hearts of mankind,
tongue-tripped into articulate words, formed and
    filled with breath,
flowing like the sea, but from
    sea-depths of meaning,

light to the eyes and
sweet relief to the heart.

Then out from that circle,
the sound of all human speech, words of
    admonition, snatches of
        conversation, starlight of
God's Compassion sprinkled throughout it,
Turkish bursts, Arabic stutter, a child's distant cry,
then roar again, sea-surf,
silence,
silence above all, and the
    twelve-dimensional
        echo of that silence.
Then a phrase of Urdu, Pashtu, Malay,
low rumble of
Qur'an recitation, pauses, people
    looking around, metallic
        clatter from far away, the
rhythmic supplications of a group of pilgrims

circling God's House.

Then the click sound of a microphone in sonic superspace
turning on.

Then words enveloped by the Word,

the Word enveloped in a roar,

the roar enveloped in silence,

the articulate silence of God, then

the silence of silence.

Then the echo of that silence.

Then the looking around.

12/26

JABAL NUR & THE CAVE OF HIRA

As an expedition, many of us had wanted to climb Jabal Nur, to visit the cave where the Prophet, peace and blessings of Allah be upon him, was visited by Gabriel and received the Qur'an and the Order from Allah to deliver His Message.

This hill is just on the outskirts of Mecca, the highest hill in the desolate landscape, shaped like a camel's hump, very steep and said to be a treacherous climb. My enthusiasm was mitigated by the danger of the climb and my fears of not being up to it. A friend who lives in Mecca, and who can see the mountain out one of the windows of his house, said that looking at it from afar was good enough, it is not a holy place in itself, and the Prophet himself never indicated that it was a place to visit. He suggested that I do the prayer of *'Istikhara,* or asking for guidance, to see if I should make the journey or not.

I did the two rakats of prayer right before turning in to sleep, asked Allah according to the Sunnah of the Prophet, and lay down on my right side, with my right hand under my cheek, expecting an answer.

My dream was as follows: A poetry reading. A poet was getting up to read. Over to my right in the room, sitting in a corner with his coterie, was a blond, British poet of renown (in the dream at least) and some skill. When the reader in the middle of the room began to read, this British poet stood up and began reciting the lines:

> *Time drops, and then soon*
> *black answers appear.*
> *Not like the first mate's charts...*

He recited so loudly that he interrupted the reader, and his attitude was one of intentional anarchy. I stood up and started shouting to him that his poetry was good enough that he didn't have to resort to cheap theatrics, and that he should shut up and let the featured poet read his poems.

The British poet kept on repeating his lines, *"Time drops, and then soon black answers appear. Not like the first mate's charts"* in an eloquent English accent, over and over again, until finally I woke up from the dream, remembering them.

Later that day, in the Meccan market, shopping with my son who was looking for a garish shirt as a kind of joke for his college roommate, going through boxes of cheap and truly outlandish shirts, I came across a kind of collage print, with photos of sailors and nautical charts, and fragments of writing on ripped pieces of paper arranged in the pattern, and suddenly I noticed these words, like black answers, appearing in readable order in the cut-up style of William Burroughs:

> *Spyglass hill*
> *rough makeup for a lack of*
> *small green.*

We later decided that the trip was too dangerous, too steep and too rough for our ill-equipped band of children and three not-completely fit older men, up a divinely meaningful spyglass hill (the revelation of Qur'an a true lens onto reality), in a barren terrain in which this remarkable protuberance, in the landscape as well as in our psychic world environment, was a rough makeup that more than made up for a lack of small green.

VISION OF THE SHARIAT

At the Prophet's Mosque in Medina I had a vision of the *Shariat* (sacred law) of Islam as a giant, spectacular many-faceted chandelier of hundreds of prisms or lenses, a kind of glittering dome of raw starlight that fits down perfectly over the *Haqiqat* (sacred truth), so that its light shines out from each lens, perfectly focused, a lens or cluster of lenses beaming the light for every aspect of our lives.

One can approach the *Haqiqat* without it, and in some cases get it right, but with the Prophet's *Shariat* from Allah, peace and blessings of Allah be upon him, the light of the *Haqiqat* can shine out clearly and one can approach the *Haqiqat* from outside with clear precision.

The lenses are such things as how to do the prayer, the proper way to contract a marriage, the laws of inheritance, etc., all the details of our lives down to things as mundane as cleaning the teeth, as well as preparing us for the rapturous experience of face-to-face meeting with Allah with correct spiritual courtesy at the highest station.

WHAT ARE FEET FOR?

What are feet for
  but to go around the Ka'ba?

What are eyes for
  but to look upon God's House?

What are lips for
  but to kiss the Black Stone?

What are hands for
  but to supplicate our Lord?

What's the heart for
  but to open to His Light?

12/27

GOD'S MADMAN

1

I saw a majdhub* at the Ka'ba
 and *Oh*, was he crazy!
He took old men's canes and
  threw them on the ground in the
path of people doing *tawaf*
then paraded back and forth jubilantly,
   crazy eyes gleaming.

He walked off in people's sandals,
 gesturing, crying out in
   hoarse, weird Arabic
phrases repeated
  over and over. He was

about thirty, black hair, unruly
 beard, wiry, intense, oh
   very intensely laughing and
insistently repeating things to a
 crowd both
  visible and invisible that
seemed to ignore him — *God's clown!*

He shuffled past in lady's shoes.
He was courteously escorted away by one of the
 guards. Later he

---

majdhub = A God-enraptured one

sauntered by in a different robe, white
   cap and
     shoes altogether, momentarily
pinched from someone, still
muttering to himself. In front of

God's House! Ecstatically
      rambunctious. Handsome,
more radiant than most. Fashioned directly from
       God's hands. Let loose
   among us. Out of control. But

not altogether: I saw him
walk past with an open
   Qur'an in one hand as if
     making a point,
waving his free arm, insisting on
   something unknown to me in his
crazy discourse to
     no one listening. I feared he might
throw the Qur'an down as he did the
   canes and sandals, but
majdhubs are directly under God's command —
   he was bodily

guarding the Word of God. He may have been
exhorting us to do so.
   Starry eyes zigzagging back and forth
     pouring light. Then

   turning his head and

laughing!

2

What is attraction to God? The *majdhub* is
    attracted to Allah with all
restraints removed, drawn magnetically,
tossing all scruples away, actually tossing his
    resistance more than his
  scruples, he's beyond

scruples, though some may be
even more scrupulous than the scholars about
   every little thing,
fearful in the Majestic Presence of Allah that one
detail of the Prophet's Sunna be neglected, one
    thought be
  out of line —
that's their "craziness." Others

to God's Beauty go, like flocks of doves in
   twilight, they laugh and sing
    enthusiastically, weep and
lament, laugh and cry, in
   crazy spirals of God's love.

Who knows what's
going on in their hearts.

He knows! That's

all they care about.

The moon reflected in a
pan of piss: God's Light in
    this world!

The delicate petals of a hidden
  blue flower unfurling.

Beetles black as Ethiopian princes
passing on a black rock
    in the black of night.

Love expressed in an instant like a
  tight-rope flung across the
    Grand Canyon and
      stepped out on,
high above silver clouds, first time
    without teetering...

Rumi said: *If you want God's Love
don't turn your back to the sun.*

These mad flotsams ride waves
    eternally beating our
  shores. They let themselves be
pushed and lifted
    by God alone.

They love the Light.

12/28

TWO SHORT POEMS

1

White moth on the
   black cloth of the Ka'ba —
Do you know where you are?

2

I had a vision
everyone circumambulating the Ka'ba
turned into tiny white birds
   and flew away.

12/28

THE MIRACLE OF PAIN

With blisters the size of Brazil
and headaches the size of Manhattan —
why is spiritual pursuit so associated with
    physical pain?

Abd al-Qadir Jilani used to
tie his hair to a nail on the wall to
snap his head back if he dozed off
        reading Qur'an.
Christian mystics endure endless permutations of
    difficulty, including spontaneously
        bleeding from the
wounds of Christ.
Sitting in Buddhist meditation on puffy black cushions
    crosslegged for hours to
focus the mind nearly
        drove me up the wall I was facing.

Birth is no picnic. Death often
    less so. Life in between: a
tough love event.

Yet it all brings us to God.

These blisters on feet around
    Ka'ba marble
around and around,
the headache that comes from
        odd short hours of
    sleep in order to

wake up the heart before Allah in the
last watches of the night —
    the abode of lovers —

is the price to pay for *ma'rifa**

as all creatures of this earth must
crack open the shells on acorns or mussels to get
    the meat, the
earth splits apart revealing
  deep fissures of ruby, whole
generations drown and later generations
    come — a

tear of joy forms in the eye of one
  who sees *The One Who*
    Sees.

12/28

**ma'rifa* = *Recognition of the Divine Reality.*

ENUMERATIONS

Eyeglass cases, brass knuckles, antelope horns,
   things that go "boom!",
umbrella stands, washboard music, broken
      combs, tombs of saints,
distant galaxies, nearby star-clusters,
   Chinese cosmologies, Custer's Last Stand,
cigarette ads, hospital wards, blender-motors,
      brass bedsteads,
iconography in red and black lacquer,
  band-aids for elephants, microphones for
      dwarves,
plastic surgery, open-heart surgery, basic dentures,
  orthopaedic socks,
blankets for thoroughbreds, houses for sale,
automobiles powered by water, sinks,
things we can see and things imagined,
full conversations and snatches of sentences,
aether, fire, earth, air and wood,
all of this is other-than-Allah and
    vanishes.

The Ka'ba sits with its black cloth cover,
is none of the above,
it too will perish.

Only Allah sustains and nourishes us
after whirlwind and smoke have
    done their job.
Our slender skeletons in folds of asbestos

may smile their skeletal smiles unknown,
but our hearts in our souls and our
    innermost secrets
fly straight to Allah on the
    backs of green birds!

Let it all go, let go of everything,
let Allah do it, it's
    His in the end.

The sweetness of life is in seeing His Presence
in the nod or the smile of a face full of light!

12/29

PRAYER AT THE KA'BA

Oh Lord, the orange cat lying asleep on the
  shoe rack outside the Ka'ba
    looked tranquil, lean from
  living wild in Mecca, but still
     cat-like and sweet-faced —
surely some of this peacefulness
    could come to me?

Oh Lord, You raise up giant roof-beams in the
  world and
    hurl great foundations
      as deep as the seas —
I am only your creation of
    flesh and bone,
  but surely some of those
    depths and heights
      could be mine?

Oh Allah, I sit here facing Your House on
  earth, beseeching Your Grace,
    seeking Your Face,
      my own not good enough in
        this life,
my own face a combination of
  lusty panther and
    awkward ostrich
    in this life,

yet I'm grateful for its

miraculous properties in
      facing the world,
especially the eyes — close them
  and light spreads,
    open them and
        miracles appear —

especially Your stark square of black cloth rising
endlessly up into the night in front of me now
    but Your Face, Lord,
      could I catch a
    glimpse of it at least?

A white owl flies in the night somewhere,
its impassive face and saucer eyes
fleeing through the air.

Is this my face, Lord,
searching everywhere?

12/20

MORE FEET

Sitting facing the Ka'ba
  like a flat black kite
    bobbing in the wind, or rather
the flat black square of the kite is
  stationary, the world is
      bobbing —
a thousand billion feet stride past, going from
left to right, feet of whole
nations it seems, feet hitting cold marble,
heels and toes passing endlessly,
feet of emperors (who knows?), feet of accountants, feet of
  women filled with grief,
feet of brand new innocent children, small and
    eager,
all shapes and colors and sizes of feet
in stately human procession,
feet seen and feet unseen, feet maybe
  of the dead, not knowing they're
    dead, sometimes only
one to a customer, sometimes none, ghost feet
  passing always to the right
taking their owners in blissful bewilderment
around their own hearts,
black kite as still as the
  deepest pillars of the
    world, the world
bobbing in the wind. Finally

    cast free!

12/30

THE MORNING OF THE LAST DAY

*Allah elects from whomever he wants of
His slaves for the presence of isolation*
— Shaykh ibn al-Habib of Fez

The sun is rising and the sky is lightening from
   deep black to fluffy blue and gray
    with shadows and tinges of white,
revealing the marble minarets like
   giant chess pieces against the sky,
the mosque's arches within arches lit by a golden
   glow around the edges
and the invincible House of Allah at the center
    covered with its cloth of endless
      night out of which the
Word of God emerges constantly in filigreed
   gold lettering around the circumference,
the round circumference of the
   square House of Allah
under a sky that brightens as I write
and is now a light blue with a puzzle of
   gray clouds moving slowly across it.

I am seated in the first row of carpets
   in front of the Ka'ba.
Behind me to my left there is a discourse in Arabic
   to unseen listeners.
To my right someone is reciting Qur'an, and
   two men with deep voices are engaged in
earnest conversation. An

African in pure white robe and
turban to my immediate left silently
    studies the Holy Book.
People pass and people sit, men and
women learning each minute the
    arduous delights of submission.

The sound in the distance now of a
marble-polishing machine, a
    steady whirr as the
    circular brush buffs places so many
thousands of human feet press,

and I am devastated and alone,
my heart a tub of molten lead
    about to pour into space.
I am lost with nowhere to go, feeling
orphaned and childless, friendless, bereft,
    a fool, constantly
imbibing my own foolishness rather than the
sweet deep spring of Allah —

I've hit zero.

The sky turned gray while I said this,
the electric lights will soon go out,
two swallows cross the gray sky,
an old beardless man in long black cape
    walks past from left to right —
is he also devastated and alone? Does he also feel
    childless, friendless? He smiles as he

passes, accompanied by a
      younger man. Another soul
lost in the cosmos? Another adrift on God's

surf?

There's no time left for fancy thoughts.

The Ka'ba faces us with its
   implacable face.

We face Allah with our
original face.

1/1/96

LAST TAWAF

On my last tawaf of the Ka'ba just before
   maghrib on the day we
     left Mecca,
I spotted the tiny old man I'd seen going
    around the Ka'ba almost
every time I'd gone there — in the middle of the
   night, just before *fajr*, just after *fajr*,
     in the afternoon —
and decided to do what I'd wanted to do one
morning, but lost him in the crowd: *Follow him!*
Learn how he does it. This

frail old man, looks like he comes from
Khazakhstan, flat
oriental face with straight straggly white beard,
blind in right eye, turban with tail
    wound around
cap, cream-colored old man's
   sweater open in front, white
     robe to his feet, ratty black socks,
wrinkled neck with shaggy
   gray hair streaked with black,
gnarled hands
patiently tapping a
    bamboo cane in front of him,

so I fall back behind him on my
first round, I slow my pace to his
snail's pace, and together we

go around the Ka'ba.

The crowd suddenly seems impetuous,
    greedy, full of
overblown bravado in all their
youth and good health, booming full-
throated recitations, passionate
    energy. He makes no

sound but the tap-tapping of his cane, his
head swivels from side to side as if he's doing
silent *dhikr* inside, or
because of his right eye, checking his
position as he goes —

people bump into him, he's a
    cork on the surf —

quietly determined he heads into the
crowd at the Yemeni corner and
touches it, I'm right behind him, he
    heads back out
and sets off for the corner of the
    Black Stone and I'm
expecting a miracle, the mad crush of
    people become suddenly savage to
kiss the Black Stone
  to open gently for him,
    but when he
gets to the black line in the marble marking the
    Black Stone's position a few yards from the

corner he
calmly turns and salutes it and
goes on.

We do six circuits this way,
very slowly, with great concentration, and I

notice that occasionally men stuff riyals into his
   sweater pocket as they pass him, he
takes one out almost astonished and
squints at it, then stuffs it back in.
This happens about three times in all.

Then on my seventh *tawaf* at the
Black Stone he must be finished, having
   started one circuit before
      me, and after greeting the Black Stone the
same way as before he
heads left into the
crowd at the gold Ka'ba door with the same
      implacable calm, and I
am free to finish on my own.

It's as if I've been propelled by a
   booster rocket that's
      dropped off.
Even at my
   slow pace, with him no longer in
front of me, my gait seems
      supersonically faster as I
         make my last round.

I had slowed myself down behind him.

I had geared down my impetuous desire for Allah,
    my rush to His Light,
my impatient greed for God's blessing
and took it easy behind him, let
everything go, no need to
    rush — Allah is everywhere, Allah is
    not locatable in time or space —

and saw how wild the world is,
men and women who passed us
    so hot compared to this
tranquil cork on the water.

Will he go round the Ka'ba like this until he
drops dead and is carried in on a green
cloth-covered bier for the
    funeral prayer?

Around and around on those
tiny socked feet, tapping his
cane,

so content with Allah,
so filled with saintly patience.

1/3

LETTER TO MANKIND

I have been to the center of the earth.
Jules Verne didn't get it right.
It's not down in cavernous bowels of igneous
  rock swathed in
    sulfurous fumes.
The serpents of the self and its idolized distractions
  are the only monsters to
    come at you out of the rocks.

I have been to the Ka'ba at Mecca
as pure as a heartbeat, as stunning in time and
space as a precious diamond decreed by God to be
  cut by the hand of man to
  mirror His Glory.

All is clarity there, and concentration.

The ears are filled with a joyous noise.

The eyes behold God's plan in the
masses of humanity that pass there that
reduce in every case to one: One heart before
One God in one moment in time,
the most public place on earth for the
most private encounter with our
    Lord.

I've sat among its people, I've
stood in the first rows of prayer facing

the House, black cloth covering
   stone,
I've bowed and prostrated as
swallows wheel in a
  sky so saturated with
light as to scintillate with a jagged
   indelible brightness.

This is still man's major crossroad.

Around the Ka'ba even the worst of men
   for a while
      regain their innocence
    and are renewed.
If they are lost in awe and tears flow and they
   call on Allah with each heartbeat
they are in Paradise.
If they walk around the House of Allah
   chatting and distracted they are
still in God's Garden, so powerful is the
     presence there.

The Ka'ba is of a
blackness that is not black, of a
   dimension that has no
     size, of a
cubeness that has no
   shape in space,
neither size, shape nor color define it,
yet it is
   such-and-such a dimension in

roughly cube shape with a
golden door set in its side and a
golden rainspout over one edge at top
made of square blocks of gray stone caulked with
   white and
covered over with fine black brocade to the ground
   embroidered at top with
golden calligraphy of God's Word.

Inside it is empty.
(I was there one morning when they
   rolled a wooden stairway to the
  door and opened it and the
    crowd came to a halt and
  gasped, and many of us
     burst into tears — I nearly
was able to enter, but
dignitaries and pilgrims with special
  green cards were the
    only ones allowed —
but I saw men in the darkness inside
face the inner wall and do the prayer,
prostrating to Allah from inside facing out in the
    holy space we pray towards
      every day *outside facing in!*)

White and pearly gray marble slabs make a
floor from the Ka'ba to the edge of the
mosque courtyard for the millions of
feet to pace, even the feet of
  cats, lean felines of Mecca, one seen

doing the seven prescribed circuits, a
   perfect pilgrim of a cat,
before wandering off among the human
   multitudes.

Faces float forward from the faces we
   bear until I think all the
faces on earth are present there,
even unbelievers, even non-Muslims
   represented by the
intensity in the faces of those
who go around God's House —
no one on earth ignored by God, no one
   not brushed by
   angels' wings, no one
in this creation of His
left in utter desolation, but is
   sustained and
conveyed into His
   Presence.

This is the heart of the world.

The self of the human.

The spirit of our consciousness in
   life and death.

Distinctions blurred and distinctions
   sharpened at the same time.

Heavens rolled up, seas
dried, earth-prints erased.

No one's gone anywhere.
No one's done anything. No one's

taken a step or even the minutest
breathtaking space of separation
    away from the

House of Allah at the

center of the earth of mankind in

space in Mecca in what is now Saudi Arabia

January 6, 1996,

Philadelphia, Pennsylvania, the United

    States of America,

3:25 a.m. one cold winter morning

in my bed on earth

at the feast of our Lord.

ABOUT THE AUTHOR

Born in 1940 in Oakland, California, Daniel Abdal-Hayy Moore's first book of poems, *Dawn Visions*, was published by Lawrence Ferlinghetti of City Lights Books, San Francisco, in 1964, and the second in 1972, *Burnt Heart/Ode to the War Dead*. He created and directed *The Floating Lotus Magic Opera Company* in Berkeley, California in the late 60s, and presented two major productions, *The Walls Are Running Blood,* and *Bliss Apocalypse*. He became a Sufi Muslim in 1970, performed the Hajj in 1972, and lived and traveled throughout Morocco, Spain, Algeria and Nigeria, landing in California and publishing *The Desert is the Only Way Out,* and *Chronicles of Akhira* in the early 80s (Zilzal Press). Residing in Philadelphia since 1990, in 1996 he published *The Ramadan Sonnets* (Jusoor/City Lights), and in 2002, *The Blind Beekeeper* (Jusoor/ Syracuse University Press). He has been the major editor for a number of works, including *The Burdah* of Shaykh Busiri, translated by Shaykh Hamza Yusuf, and the poetry of Palestinian poet, Mahmoud Darwish, translated by Munir Akash. He is also widely published on the worldwide web: *The American Muslim, DeenPort,* and his own website: www.danielmoorepoetry.com; and poetry blog: www.ecstaticxchange.wordpress.com, among others. He is also currently literary editor for *Seasons Journal* and editor for *State of Siege* by Mahmoud Darwish, published by Syracuse University Press. The Ecstatic Exchange Series is bringing out the extensive body of his works of poetry (a complete list of published works on page 2).

POETIC WORKS by Daniel Abdal-Hayy Moore
Published and Unpublished
(many by, or soon to be by, *The Ecstatic Exchange*)

Dawn Visions (published by City Lights, 1964)
Burnt Heart/Ode to the War Dead (published by City Lights, 1972)
This Body of Black Light Gone Through the Diamond (printed by Fred
    Stone, Cambridge, Mass, 1965)
On The Streets at Night Alone (1965?)
All Hail the Surgical Lamp (1967)
States of Amazement (1970)

Abdallah Jones and the Disappearing-Dust Caper (published by The
    Ecstatic Exchange/Crescent Series, 2006)
'Ala ud-Deen and the Magic Lamp
The Chronicles of Akhira (1981) (published by Zilzal Press with
    Typoglifs by Karl Kempton, 1986; collected in Sparrow on the
    Prophet's Tomb, by The Ecstatic Exchange, 2009)
Mouloud (1984) (A Zilzal Press chapbook, 1995; collected in Sparrow on
    the Prophet's Tomb, by The Ecstatic Exchange, 2009)
Man is the Crown of Creation (1984)
The Look of the Lion (The Parabolas of Sight) (1984)
The Desert is the Only Way Out (completed 4/21/84) (Zilzal Press
    chapbook, 1985)
Atomic Dance (1984) (am here books, 1988)
Outlandish Tales (1984)
Awake as Never Before (12/26/84) (Zilzal Press chapbook, 1993)
Glorious Intervals (1/1/85) (Zilzal Press chapbook, ?)
Long Days on Earth/Book I (1/28 – 8/30/85)
Long Days on Earth/Book II (Hayy Ibn Yaqzan)
Long Days on Earth/Book III (1/22/86)
Long Days on Earth/Book IV (1986)
The Ramadan Sonnets (Long Days on Earth/Book V) (5/9 – 6/11/86)
    (Published by Jusoor/City Lights Books, 1996) (Republished as
    Ramadan Sonnets by The Ecstatic Exchange, 2005)
Long Days on Earth/Book VI (6-8/30/86)
Holograms (9/4/86 – 3/26/87)

History of the World (The Epic of Man's Survival) (4/7 – 6/18/87)

Exploratory Odes (6/25 – 10/18/87)

The Man at the End of the World (11/11 – 12/10/87)

The Perfect Orchestra (3/30 – 7/25/88) (Published by The Ecstatic Exchange, 2009)

Fed from Underground Springs (7/30 – 11/23/88)

Ideas of the Heart (11/27/88 – 5/5/89)

New Poems (scattered poems, from 3/24 – 8/9/89)

Facing Mecca (5/16 – 11/11/89)

A Maddening Disregard for the Passage of Time (11/17/89 – 5/20/90)

The Heart Falls in Love with Visions of Perfection (6/15/90 – 6/2/91)

Like When You Wave at a Train and the Train Hoots Back at You (Farid's Book) (6/11 – 7/26/91) (Published by The Ecstatic Exchange, 2008)

Orpheus Meets Morpheus (8/1/91– 3/14/92)

The Puzzle (3/21/92 – 8/17/93)

The Greater Vehicle (10/17/93 – 4/30/94)

A Hundred Little 3-D Pictures (5/14/94 – 9/11/95)

The Angel Broadcast (9/29 – 12/17/95)

Mecca/Medina Time-Warp (12/19/95 – 1/6/96) (Published as a Zilzal Press chapbook, 1996, collected in Sparrow on the Prophet's Tomb, by The Ecstatic Exchange, 2009)

Miracle Songs for the Millennium (1/20 – 10/16/96)

The Blind Beekeeper (11/15/96 – 5/30/97) (Published 2002 by Jusoor/ Syracuse University Press)

Chants for the Beauty Feast (6/3 – 10/28/97)

You Open a Door and it's a Starry Night (10/29/97 – 5/23/98) (Published by The Ecstatic Exchange, 2009)

Salt Prayers (5/29 – 10/24/98) (Published by The Ecstatic Exchange, 2005)

Some (10/25/98 – 4/25/99)

Flight to Egypt (5/1 – 5/16/99)

I Imagine a Lion (5/21 – 11/15/99) (Published by The Ecstatic Exchange, 2006)

Millennial Prognostications (11/25/99 – 2/2/2000) (Published by the Ecstatic Exchange, 2009)

Shaking the Quicksilver Pool (2/4 – 10/8/2000) (Published by The Ecstatic Exchange, 2009)

Blood Songs (10/9/2000 – 4/3/2001)

The Music Space (4/10 – 9/16/2001) (Published by The Ecstatic Exchange, 2007)

Where Death Goes (9/20/2001 – 5/1/2002) (Published by The Ecstatic Exchange, 2009)

The Flame of Transformation Turns to Light (99 Ghazals Written in English) (5/14 – 8/21/2002) (Published by The Ecstatic Exchange, 2007)

Through Rose-Colored Glasses (7/22/2002 – 1/15/2003) (Published by The Ecstatic Exchange, 2007)

Psalms for the Broken-Hearted (1/22 – 5/25/2003) (Published by The Ecstatic Exchange, 2006)

Hoopoe's Argument (5/27 – 9/18/03)

Love is a Letter Burning in a High Wind (9/21 – 11/6/2003) (Published by The Ecstatic Exchange, 2006)

Laughing Buddha/Weeping Sufi (11/7/2003 – 1/10/2004) (Published by The Ecstatic Exchange, 2005)

Mars and Beyond (1/20 – 3/29/2004) (Published by The Ecstatic Exchange, 2005)

Underwater Galaxies (4/5 – 7/21/2004) (Published by The Ecstatic Exchange, 2007)

Cooked Oranges (7/23/2004 – 1/24/2005 (Published by The Ecstatic Exchange, 2007)

Holiday from the Perfect Crime (1/25 – 6/11/2005)

Stories Too Fiery to Sing Too Watery to Whisper (6/13 – 10/24/2005)

Coattails of the Saint (10/26/2005 – 5/10/2006) (Published by The Ecstatic Exchange, 2006)

In the Realm of Neither (5/14/2006 – 11/12/06) (Published by The Ecstatic Exchange, 2008)

Invention of the Wheel (11/13/06 – 6/10/07)

The Sound of Geese Over the House (6/15 – 11/4/07)

The Fire Eater's Lunchbreak (11/11/07 – 5/19/2008) (Published by The Ecstatic Exchange, 2008)

Sparks Off the Main Strike (5/24/2008 – 1/10/2009)

Stretched Out on Amethysts (1/13/2009 –)

www.ingramcontent.com/pod-product-compliance
Lightning Source LLC
Chambersburg PA
CBHW020855090426
42736CB00008B/386